America's Hidden Heroes

America's Hidden Heroes
The History and Evolution
of U.S. Navy Frogmen and SEALs

By
Commander (SEAL) Tom Hawkins, USN, Retired

To Cheryl

Tom Hawkins

PHOCA
Press ✦ LLC

To Cheryl

Sam Harris

America's Hidden Heroes

www.PhocaPress.com/Hidden-Heroes -US-Navy-SEAL-History

Copyright © 2015 Tom Hawkins

PHOCA

Press ✥ L L C

Published by Phoca Press
New York, NY 10025
www.PhocaPress.com

Phoca Press publishes works by, for, and about the Naval Special Warfare community. Our mission is to enhance the public's appreciation and understanding of the contributions of the Naval Special Warfare community through history up to today.

ISBN-13: 978-0-9909153-0-0-1-7

10 9 8 7 6 5 4 3 2

The National Navy SEAL Museum is pleased to support publication of *America's Hidden Heroes: The History and Evolution of U.S. Navy Frogmen and SEALs.*

When a Basic Underwater Demolition/SEAL (BUD/S) graduate advances to SEAL Tactical Training and after that to an active-duty SEAL Team, he takes with him the heart of the Navy SEAL *Ethos:* "Brave men have fought and died building the proud tradition and feared reputation that I am bound to uphold. In the worst of conditions, the legacy of my teammates steadies my resolve and silently guides my every deed."

The Navy SEAL Museum's mission is to promote public education by providing the opportunity to explore the history and heritage of Naval Special Warfare. This book brings together into one volume their storied history of heroism and service. As the only museum solely dedicated to preserving the history of the Navy SEALs and their predecessors, we especially value the concise insight this book brings to its readers.

It is only fitting that our nation's newest SEALs come to know that legacy. We are pleased to present a copy of this book to every man that graduates from BUD/S, which remains the toughest training in the military.

HooYa!

Rick Kaiser
Executive Director

"We were ready to do what nobody else could do, and what nobody else wanted to do."

UDT Lieutenant Ted Fielding, Korea 1950

"On any given day, Navy SEALs can be operating in more than 40 countries. In some areas we are asked to be there; in other areas people don't want us there; in some other areas they don't know we are there; and in some parts of the world people think we are there, but we have never operated there."

Rear Admiral (SEAL) Garry J. Bonelli

"Not gold, but only men can make a people great and strong; men who for truth and honor's sake, stand fast and suffer long. Brave men, who work while others sleep, who dare while others fly—they build a nation's pillars deep and lift them to the sky."

Ralph Waldo Emerson

Contents

Author's Forward:
Legacy of Heroes

The Navy does not order men to join the U.S. Navy SEAL Teams. Each person freely chooses to put himself through this arduous duty, where the routine is extreme, and danger and hardship are faced every day. From the early days of the Second World War into the conflicts around the world today, exceptional men willingly step forward for the toughest assignments, and many have given their all in the ultimate sacrifice.

What kind of man does this?

How did this unique maritime force get started?

What separates the U.S. Navy's elite commandos from all others?

Four units formed during World War II are the formidable legacy units of today's Navy SEALs. Modern operators can trace their capabilities and origins to the:

- **Amphibious Scouts and Raiders (S&R)**: Established in August 1942 for European commando operations and amphibious reconnaissance

- **Naval Combat Demolition Units (NCDUs)**: These Demolitioneers started training in May and June 1943 to clear beaches and harbors of obstacles in Italy, Normandy's Utah and Omaha beaches, and the coast of Southern France.

- **Underwater Demolition Teams (UDTs)**: Our country's first combat swimmers began in December 1943, with missions that included hydrographic reconnaissance and obstacle demolition in advance of amphibious landings throughout the Pacific.

- **Office of Strategic Services Maritime Unit (OSS MU)**: A clandestine component of what would eventually become the CIA, these secretive boat crews and combat divers operated clandestinely in Europe, Asia, and with the Pacific UDTs.

In addition to these significant groups, a number of other units and organizations formed during the war contributed to America's maritime commando capabilities.

Today's Naval Special Warfare Command includes U.S. Navy SEALs, Special Warfare Combatant-Craft Crewmen (SWCC), and a host of mission-enablers that remain an essential component of conflicts worldwide, including the war against terrorism.

While making headlines today, most of their history has been purposely obscured. With obscurity comes some degree of security in a very dangerous business. During the last decade, Navy SEALs have become a generally undesired public sensation with the daring rescue of the captain of the *Maersk Alabama* Richard Phillips, the killing of Osama bin Laden during the enterprising raid at Abbottabad, Pakistan, the audacious rescue of Jessica Buchanan, and countless movies, books, and video games.

The very best of men humbly and silently served and never sought to publicize their achievements or profit from their exploits. Unlike the glamorous image presented in media today, most SEALs remain "silent professionals" in the best tradition of the men of the Scouts and Raiders, Naval Combat Demolition Units, Underwater Demolition Teams, and the OSS Maritime Unit. They embody the essence of courage, judgment, integrity and dedication.

SEAL Team Two, 7th Platoon – Vietnam: June 1970 - Dec 1970 – Kneeling (l-r): LT Thomas. L. Hawkins (CTE 116.0.1.3), IC1 Edward J. McQueen, BM1 James R. Owens (MST). Standing: EM2 Guntis J. Jaunzems, ETN2 Carl T. Zellers, BM1 James F. Finley, LDNN, SFP2 Joseph M. Silva, GMGC Mike Spencer, LTJG Robert M. Rieve, SFP2 Frederick J. Keener, HM1 Charles P. O'Bryan. Back: EN2 Lester Oakman (MST), GMG2 Dennis H. Johnson, BM2 Michael L. Naus, QM3 William K. Day. Not in the photograph: BM1 William A. McCarthy.

Chapter 1:
World War II

The Lines on the World Map 1942

When the Japanese bombed Pearl Harbor 7 December 1942 in Hawaii, they launched a western Pacific offensive that encompassed an invasion of the Philippine Islands. The European War expanded into World War II with Germany's declaration of war on the United States. The world aligned into two massive warfighting machines. Germany, Japan and Italy formed the Axis powers. The United States and the British Commonwealth lead the Allied powers. Small states chose one side or the other, putting nearly the entire world at war.

The attack on Pearl Harbor destroyed most of the U.S. Pacific Fleet, leaving unchallenged command of the Pacific to the Japanese. The crippled American forces could do little but stand and watch Imperial Japan gobble up the Philippines; followed by Guam and New Guinea, the Solomon Islands, and nearly every other island chain in the western Pacific.

The lines on the map of the world in early spring 1942 must have been discouraging for allied military planners. The challenge facing the Allies to defeat the Axis powers was daunting. In Europe, every inch of non-communist territory and the majority of North Africa were under German and Italian control. Everything west of the International Dateline and south to the Coral Sea was in Japanese hands. Destroying the Axis would take an unprecedented effort. Assaulting the beaches in Europe would require an amphibious force of a scale never before imagined, and with capabilities not yet conceived.

The U.S. Navy began expansion of its Amphibious Forces early in 1942. They established a series of Amphibious Training Bases (ATBs) on the East Coast and along the coast of California. These new bases focused on training men, the officers who would lead them, and on the skills needed for massive seaborne invasions. Within the Amphibious Forces, special mission units that were the precursors to U.S. Navy SEALs were formed: the S&Rs, NCDUs, UDTs, and others. At the same time, the OSS was forming its Maritime Unit by culling qualified volunteers from the Marines, Navy, Army, and the U.S. Coast Guard.

The Allies were not alone in thinking about attacks from the sea. Italy's navy already had commando units trained and operating underwater and with surface attacks using small combatants. Equipped with early devices for breathing underwater, Italian combat divers had proven they could infiltrate enemy harbors using a specially modified torpedo, plant explosives, and sink or severely damage British ships.

These audacious Italian naval commandos were part of the "Decima Flottiglia Mas," the 10th Light Assault Flotilla, and worked closely with other secretive units such as Gamma. They successfully attacked British ships at Alexandria, Egypt and Gibraltar. When the British figured out how the Italians were attacking, they were frantic to develop their own underwater capabilities and equipment. U.S. military and intelligence leaders saw similar value in underwater commandos, and were equally desperate to find, train, and equip such men.

Amphibious Scouts and Raiders

Atlantic Operations

The Scouts and Raiders (S&R), intended for operations in Europe, trained at ATB Little Creek, Virginia for reconnaissance missions against potential landing beaches and for leading assault forces to assigned positions while under the cover of darkness. The S&R training included men from Army and Navy units. Navy officers and sailors were drawn from the boat pool at ATB, Solomons, Maryland. Army officers and soldiers volunteered from the 3rd and 9th Infantry Divisions. The first deployable unit was formed in August 1942, and was led by commanding officer Army 1st Lieutenant Lloyd Peddicord with Navy Ensign John Bell serving as executive officer. The men trained side-by-side before shipping out to North Africa.

Amphibious Scouts and Raiders training with inflatable boats.

In November 1942, during Operation TORCH at Morocco, in North Africa, Scout and Raider commandos launched from the submarine *USS Barb* (SS-220) in kayaks, and this was the first wartime submarine-based operation involving U.S. reconnaissance personnel. The S&R men paddled their inflatable boats in total darkness until they reached the Jette Principal at the harbor opening at Safi. Once there, they guided two destroyers, the *USS Cole* (DD-155) and the *USS Bernadou* (DD-153), into the harbor without the ships being detected. The French defenders didn't notice enemy ships until just before 0400 the following morning. By then, it was too late. Control of the port proved important when the Vichy French, on the side of the Axis, proved willing to fight instead of the expected easy surrender.

With the success of North Africa behind them, the Scouts and Raiders changed their focus to the Mediterranean. Training was moved from ATB Little Creek to ATB Fort Pierce, Florida in February 1943 for effective year round training, since winter had settled on the Virginia Tidewater and the Chesapeake Bay.

Amphibious Scout and Raiders being launched from their host ship for daytime training. They would be taken near shore in the ship's Landing Craft Personnel, Ramp (LCPR), where they would complete their clandestine infiltration in the inflatable boats seen stacked. In a real-world mission, they would have operated under the cover of darkness.

The invasion of Sicily marked the start of the Allied assault on Nazi-occupied Europe. Code-named Operation HUSKY, the invasion of the southern end of the island on the night of 9 July 1943 was the first large-scale amphibious landing of the war on European territory. The Scouts and Raiders played essential roles in additional landings in Italy and then moved on to England to prepare for the invasion of Northern France.

Once in England, Scouts and Raiders trained side-by-side with British commandoes in advance of Operation OVERLORD, the carefully guarded amphibious assault at Normandy. Training in advance of D-Day, which occurred on 6 June 1944, included escape and evasion, operations involving submarines, and other amphibious capabilities. Members of these teams conducted extensive reconnaissance missions on the beaches, where planners hoped to land the initial waves of infantry. Weeks before the June 1944 landings, Scout and Raider men, operating with British commandos, slipped through the darkness in kayaks to collect beach samples that helped planners identify where they could best offload heavy equipment without getting mired in the sand.

The last European operation for the Scouts and Raiders was the August 1944 invasion of Southern France. Operation DRAGOON was the last amphibious assault in the European Theater. With the U.S. Seventh Army safely ashore and marching inland, the Scouts and Raiders returned to the states.

Scout and Raiders training in hand-to-hand combat at their training base in Fort Pierce, Florida.

Most of the men returned to Fort Pierce to serve as instructors at the Scout and Raider School, while others were retrained and sent to the Pacific.

Pacific Operations

A second and less-known Scouts and Raider unit was dubbed Special Services Unit #1 (SSU-1). Like its European counterpart, SSU-1 was a joint force, this time including personnel combined from the U.S. Army, Navy, and Marine Corps as well as men from the Australian Army.

The SSU men collected for training at Queensland Australia's Cairns Base on 18 July 1943. Training was comprehensive and included physical fitness, martial arts, hand-to-hand combat, making maps, operating inflatable watercraft, jungle survival, coral formation dynamics under water, sea creature identification, how to sketch panoramas and pinpoint precise locations, and even Pidgin English should they encounter natives.

WWII Amphibious Scouts and Raiders (S&R) maneuver their rubber raiding craft ashore to conduct reconnaissance and lead assault waves to a designated landing beach. (Found in the U.S. Navy Art Collection)

On 28 August, the group relocated to Fergusson Island, the largest of the D'Entrecasteaux chain off the eastern tip of New Guinea. They would see action at the Huon Peninsula campaign, which began in September, with the SSU-1 taking part in operations at Finschhafen. Additional missions included operations at Gasmata, Arawe, Cape Gloucester, and the New Guinea island of New Britain. While the teams in Europe focused on amphibious pre-assault missions, the Pacific SSU-1 Scouts and Raiders were highly involved in intelligence gathering and training, and operating with indigenous fighters using guerilla-warfare methods. The group later evolved into the 7th Amphibious Scouts and came under the command of staff intelligence sections onboard ships.

Rare photograph of SSU-1 men seen at New Guinea. The unit was composed of U.S., Australian, and indigenous forces.

In China
Upon returning from Europe, selected Scout and Raider volunteers were assigned to the U.S. Naval Group in China, where Captain Milton "Mary" Miles worked with General Tai Li, who was the military leader Generalissimo Chiang Kai-shek trusted the most. Together, they created the Sino-American Cooperative Organization (SACO), and were charged with training and equipping guerrilla forces to operate against Japanese occupiers.

Instructors at the Scout and Raider School at Fort Pierce were assigned to train Navy volunteers for planned raiding operations in China under a reshaped mission code-named "Amphibious Roger."

Admiral Ernest J. King, Chief of the U.S. Fleet and Chief of Naval Operations (CNO), planned to bolster the work of SACO by providing 120 officers and 900 men; all trained at the Scout and Raider School. Nicknamed the "Rice Paddy Navy," these Amphibious Roger men would be used for intelligence collection and raiding operations. The plan was to use these men for information gathering and raids along the Yangtze River and throughout coastal China.

Scouts and Raiders display their operational equipment at ATB, Fort Pierce.

Very few of the men trained for Amphibious Roger actually made it to China before the war ended. Those who did were used in ways quite different from teams in Europe and elsewhere in the Pacific. Their primary missions involved training Chinese guerilla fighters, reconnoitering targets, and surveying beaches for a mainland China invasion. They also reported on weather and sea conditions in their areas of operation.

Naval Combat Demolition Units

Special Mission Demolition Unit–Africa
Also in late August 1942 at Little Creek, a specialized naval demolition team was formed with two naval reserve officers and 17 enlisted men. All were U.S. Navy trained salvage divers. Their crash course included demolitions, commando tactics, cable cutting, and rubber boat training. Their single mission was to demolish a heavily-cabled boom blocking the Wadi Sebou River in Morocco. Removing this boom would allow *USS Dallas* (DD-199) to proceed up the river and train her guns on the Port Lyautey airdrome in preparation for attack by embarked Army Rangers. The cable boom was successfully destroyed, and the Rangers were able to attack and secure the airfield. This is a riveting story of determination and success, however,

the group was quickly disbanded once they returned from Africa. Because they were Navy divers, and because they were given training in demolitions, they have often been referred to as underwater demolition men, but they were not. Of interest, every man in this group was awarded the Navy Cross Medal for their actions during this mission.

ATB Solomons, Maryland: Naval Demolition Project Phase 1

Chief of Naval Operations letter Serial 01398 of 6 May 1943 established the "Naval Demolition Project," which outlined the need to "to meet a present and urgent requirement" involving amphibious operations. The project was to have two phases. As a result, the Vice Chief of Naval Operations directed the Bureau of Yards and Docks to detach eight officers and 30 enlisted men for duty with the Operational Naval Demolition Unit and Naval Demolition Unit No. 1 at the Amphibious Training Base (ATB), Solomons, Maryland. The first phase was to be under the command of Navy Commander John C. Daniel.

Inflatable boat made famous in many photographs taken at Fort Pierce. It is adorned by a logo designed by the Walt Disney Studios during World War II. A similar design can be seen in the book Disney Dons Dogtags: The Best of Disney Military Insignia From World *War II, by Walton Rawls,* © *1992 by The Walt Disney Company.*

On 14 May, six officers and 18 enlisted men from Camp Peary, Virginia arrived at Solomons for training. Camp Peary, near the town of Williamsburg, was the primary training site of the Seabees, the nickname of the Naval Construction Battalions (CBs). Once at

Solomons, the men, led by LT Fred Wise, underwent four weeks of intense instruction before shipping out to participate in the invasion of Sicily–Operation HUSKY.

Based upon the success of the first phase, Commander Daniel recommended that the Navy continue with the second phase of the project. In his 27 May report, he detailed a more complete training program and recommended equipment that an operational unit of this type would need. Additionally, he recommended that the training program should be relocated to the new ATB at Fort Pierce, Florida where, unlike at the Maryland base, training could be conducted year round.

ATB Fort Pierce, Florida:
Naval Demolition Project Phase 2

By June 1943, Commander Daniel's recommendations were put into action. The Navy tasked Lieutenant Commander Draper Kauffman to establish a Naval Combat Demolition Unit School at Fort Pierce; a training program that would eventually become legendary. LCDR Kauffman hand-picked several officers from the Bomb Disposal School in Washington, DC; a training program that he had also organized. As in Phase 1, most of the volunteers for the program came from the Seabee training school at Camp Peary. Others came from the recruit training program at Bainbridge, Maryland.

Many aspects of the current Basic Underwater Demolition/ SEAL or BUD/S training program were pioneered by LCDR Kauffman and his training staff at Fort Pierce. The institution of "Hell Week," an intense period of physical and emotional testing, remains a cornerstone of SEAL training today. Though considerably older than the men in the program, LCDR Kauffman himself trained alongside the men every chance he got.

As outlined by historians Sue Ann Dunford and James O'Dell, the NCDU project from the outset appeared to have been modeled, in part, after the British Commandos, where officers taught by example; doing exactly what was required of the enlisted men. "The British stressed the buddy system and strenuous conditioning. Their influence permeated the American effort, extending from equipment to reconnaissance technique....The British sought 'volunteers for special service' who were physically fit, good swimmers, intelligent, and self-reliant."

NCDU-114–Officer in Charge Ensign Sid Robbins is surrounded by his men. Seen seated at his left is the NCDU Training Officer Lieutenant William Flynn. This is typical of the photograph taken of each NCDU on Graduation Day at Fort Pierce.

One of those early volunteers in the first class, Seaman Bill Dawson said, "He sure earned our respect for that." The requirement that officers go through the exact same training as the enlisted men is another precedent still in place today.

Training emphasized physical fitness, swimming and diving abilities, stealth and reconnaissance, and the destruction of obstacles like those expected on European beaches from the Northern Atlantic and throughout the Mediterranean.

By the time the first training class concluded, 65 to 75% of the men had quit; a similar rate of attrition seen during the BUD/S training experience today.

LCDR Kauffman's NCDU training program contributed to creating his reputation as the "father of naval combat demolition."

UDT men placing explosive charges on beach obstacles called "Hedgehogs." These were typical of the obstacles encountered by the NCDU men at Utah and Omaha Beaches at Normandy.

The men were formed into deployable Naval Combat Demolition Units (NCDUs) at the conclusion of training in September of 1943. Each unit consisted of an officer and five enlisted men. Of the first units to graduate, several were sent to the Pacific to join the Third and Fifth Fleets. Three other units were tasked to the Mediterranean. One joined the British fleet. All units in the second class graduated the following November, and were deployed to England to participate in Operation OVERLOAD, the invasion of Normandy.

Naval Combat Demolition Units Deploy

The first NCDU from the first class at Fort Pierce actually deployed in August 1943 before completing training. The "present and urgent requirement" that drove the Chief of Naval Operations to establish the NCDU in the first place was very real. LTjg Edwin Williams and his men were sent to The Aleutian Islands Campaign, which was a struggle over this part of the Alaska Territory. A small Japanese force occupied the islands of Attu and Kiska, and this was the only U.S. territory occupied during WWII. The NCDU men were not permitted to combat while in Alaska, because the Japanese had already abandoned their positions. The men were subsequently sent to Hawaii to assist with establishment of UDT-1 and UDT-2, which were formed later that year.

It didn't take long for the NCDUs to demonstrate their worth to the top brass of the military. NCDU-4 led by Warrant Officer Ward Cartree and NCDU-5 led by Warrant Officer Ben Morris departed for the South Pacific on 8 September 1943. By 15 February 1944, both units joined with Special Services Unit-1 off the coast of New Guinea. They participated in the successful invasion of Green Island, located between New Ireland and Bougainville, and other islands off the New Guinea coast. Following these operations, they were ordered to Hawaii for advanced training and amalgamation into the UDTs being formed at Maui.

Left to Right: Dillard Williams, William Dawson, Frank Kaine, Johnny Wilhide and William Armstrong of NCDU-2 in Borneo.

LTjg Frank Kaine led NCDU-2, which worked in concert with NCDU-3 under LTjg Lloyd Anderson. These two were the first to arrive in support of the amphibious forces in the South Pacific. Their first operations were in the Admiralty Islands in March 1944. As part of the 7th Amphibious Force, they conducted reconnaissance and demolition operations throughout the area from Biak to Borneo. They would soon be joined by NCDU-19, NCDU-20 and NCDU-21, and later by NCDU-24 from Normandy. Under the overall leadership of Frank Kaine, these NCDUs rotated through operations, spreading the work evenly over 36 months and 36 operations.

Only these six units remained under the NCDU designation until the end of the war. All other NCDUs were directly integrated into the Pacific UDTs or joined the UDTs after service in Europe.

Pencil drawing displaying NCDU men at Omaha Beach, Normandy, France on D-Day, 6 June 1944 (Drawing is in the Navy Art Collection)

NCDU Units at Normandy

ATB Fort Pierce had turned out 34 NCDUs by April of 1944 destined for Operation OVERLORD. The units assembled in England to begin preparations for D-Day. Three U.S. Navy Seamen from a training pool in Scotland were assigned to each six-man NCDU. The extra manpower would help with the handling of hundreds of pounds of demolitions materiel. Four Army combat engineers joined each unit to create Gap Assault Teams of 13 men for the task of opening lanes through German obstacles to clear the way for amphibious landing craft.

The amphibious assault phase of the invasion, code named Operation NEPTUNE, called for the NCDU men and Army engineers to blow 16 gaps, each at least 50 feet wide to accommodate the follow-on waves of infantry that would be ensuing very quickly. Some planners considered the task to be close to suicidal.

The Abbot Laboratory sponsored art depicting NCDU men at work on Omaha Beach. (Found in the Navy Art Collection)

LCDR Joseph Gibbons led the NCDUs at Omaha Beach on D-Day, where the men performed admirably; however, 31 men were killed that day, with 60 wounded, resulting in a casualty rate of 52%. Still, they were able to clear eight complete lanes and two partial lanes under intense fire.

WWII Naval Combat Demolition Units (NCDUs) attacking obstacles on D-Day at Normandy, France (Found in the Navy Art Collection)

At Utah Beach, LCDR Herbert Peterson led the NCDUs that cleared 700 yards of that beach in the first two hours of the invasion, with another 900 yards cleared by the afternoon. The Utah Beach NCDUs lost six men and suffered 11 wounded. D-Day was and remains the bloodiest day in Naval Special Warfare history.

Overall Allied casualties topped 9,000, while the entrenched Germans suffered between 4,000 and 9,000. Despite the massive quantities of explosives carried and placed by the NCDU men, not a single casualty was due to improper handling. Three Presidential Unit Citations were awarded for actions that day. The NCDUs on Omaha Beach received one of them. The men at Utah Beach were awarded the Navy Unit Commendation–the only one awarded for D-Day.

Invading Southern France
NCDU men in Europe were engaged in combat once more. Reinforcements from Fort Pierce joined the men from Utah Beach for Operation DRAGOON; the code-name of the invasion of Southern France conducted in August 1944.

First code-named Operation ANVIL, the planners originally hoped the assault would happen simultaneously with the Operation NEPTUNE phase of the Normandy Invasion. Instead, it would happen two months later, making it something of a footnote of the main offensive. Though the Normandy landings were successful, that part of France had no deep water ports, and the temporary Mulberry artificial harbors were battered by storms. Though Cherbourg was liberated by the first week of July, the Germans had mined and thoroughly wrecked the harbor, rendering it nearly useless. Le Harve was still under German control.

The offensive began on 15 August and led to the capture of Toulon and Marseilles, and opened a path north up the Rhone River. After this last amphibious assault, the war in Europe became a march across land and a race to Berlin. That left no further role for the NCDUs.

While initially trying to find their mission, the NCDU men played a crucial role in the European Theatre. After their successes and return to the United States, many were folded into the Pacific Underwater Demolition Teams. Because of this, the UDTs have often been erroneously credited with the Normandy operations and the landings in southern France. During WWII, the UDTs operated only in the Pacific.

NCDU-48 photographed at ATB Fort Pierce, Florida on 26 July 1944. This unit was led by Ensign John Hunt (kneeling right).

Another common mistake has been referring to the NCDU men as "frogmen." In France, the NCDU men wore full combat dress and paddled or waded ashore to attach explosives to obstacles in the surf zones. They did not wear diving apparatus or fins.

Disaster at Tarawa

In the aftermath of the Allied victory at Guadalcanal in February 1943, planners for Allied forces in the Pacific started mapping out new offensives. General Douglas MacArthur's troops penetrated New Guinea in the north; Admiral Chester Nimitz laid plans for a campaign to take one island after another across the central Pacific. Known as the "Island-Hopping Campaign," Admiral

Nimitz planned to move against Japan by capturing one island, and then using it as a base for securing the next. The Gilbert Islands were his starting point. He planned to take the Marshalls first and next the Marianas. When these islands were secure, the U.S. would have the strategic bases needed to commence bombing Japan in advance of an all-out invasion.

The Gilbert Islands were the natural point for the beginning of the campaign, because their fortifications blocked the navigation lanes to the Marshalls and hindered shipments and communications from Hawaii. The strategic importance of this small island chain was not lost on the Japanese. They fortified the small island of Betio on the western tip of Tarawa Atoll with a maze of bunkers and trenches. The battle plan identified the airfield on Betio as the key objective. The landing strips lay east to west, with the Tarawa lagoon bordering the north side of the field. Planners put the main landing on the lagoon side of the island. Though the lagoon was shallow, planners thought the north beaches would be a better place to land than the more exposed, but deeper south side. They knew a coral reef ran about 1,200 yards from the shore. Concerns about the ability of the landing craft to make it over the reef, however, were quickly dismissed by planners, who used aerial reconnaissance reports to estimate that high tide would allow the boats to clear this potential obstacle.

The planners were wrong. With laden Marines and their weapons, the amphibious assault craft snared on the reefs and became hopelessly stuck. Intelligence planners had not realized the tide cycle was at its lowest range, and that the high tide would not be enough to allow the boats to clear the reef. Unable to drive forward or reverse off the reef, the boats were sitting ducks for Japanese gunners.

Marines had no choice but to abandon their landing craft and try to wade or swim to shore—all under relentless machine gun fire. Weighed down with weapons and heavy ammunition, those who were not shot or wounded drowned while trying to make it to shore. The Battle of "Bloody Tarawa" made it clear that the Navy could not base its plans on aerial reconnaissance alone. They needed men with the capability to accomplish pre-assault hydrographic reconnaissance for natural and man-made obstacles, and to eliminate any that could turn a potential assault beach into a disaster.

Underwater Demolition Teams

Tarawa taught Navy war planners a terrible lesson. In its aftermath, Admiral Kelley Turner, who commanded the Fifth Amphibious Force, concluded that he needed something larger than the standard NCDU, and issued a fleet-wide directive calling for 30 officers and 150 enlisted men to report to ATB Waimanalo (now known as Bellows Beach Air Force Station) on the island of Oahu, Hawaii. They would become the core of an experimental pre-assault reconnaissance and demolition program.

Admiral Turner designated the new groups "Underwater Demolition Teams" to establish an identity separate from the six-man NCDUs. Thus, UDT-1 and UDT-2 became "provisional" units, because their mission had not yet been clearly defined. Once organized on or about 1 December 1943, each UDT would have a fighting strength of 12 officers and 74 enlisted men broken down into smaller platoon sized units for command and control. UDT-1 was led by Commander Edward D. Brewster from the Seabees, and UDT-2 by Lieutenant Commander John T. Koehler, who had previously served in the Mediterranean Theater at Gela, Sicily. Their teams were made up of largely volunteers from Navy Seabee units and demolition-trained engineers from the Army and the Marine Corps, including officers. Several Fort Pierce trained NCDUs were among those assigned. The majority of Army and Marine Corps personnel were assigned to UDT-2.

With great urgency and little more than one month to train, these new UDTs quickly saw action in the Marshall Islands during Operation FLINTLOCK on 31 January 1944, which included assaults on Kwajalein and Roi-Namur. Following FLINTLOCK, the UDT men returned to Hawaii, where Army and Marine Corps personnel were returned to their parent units and the teams became all naval personnel. In February, the training was relocated to the island of Maui, where LCDR Koehler was tasked to establish a permanent training base adjacent to ATB Kamaole. This new location, known as the Naval Combat Demolition Unit Training and Experimental Base, would substantially increase the emphasis on combat swimming and mass underwater demolition operations.

WWII UDT men preparing demolitions for a forthcoming amphibious assault operation somewhere in the Pacific.

From this point forward, all UDTs were made up with the men from Fort Pierce; except UDT-14, UDT-16, and UDT-17, which were "fleet teams" formed largely from volunteers throughout the Pacific Fleet. This was because Fort Pierce training school could not meet the demand needed.

During the period September 1943 and April 1945, all of the officers and men leaving Fort Pierce retained their identity as NCDUs. Upon arrival at Maui, they were formed into 100-man UDTs and the now somewhat doctrinal operational platoons for boat and beach reconnaissance assignments. Beginning in April 1945, the men were formed in to numbered UDTs before leaving Fort Pierce.

From their beginning in December 1943 and until the end of hostilities in August 1945, the Pacific UDTs performed with valor and participated in every major amphibious assault operation from the south Pacific toward Japan; including preparations for the invasion of Japan. These major operations included: Kwajalein, Roi-Namur, Eniwetok, Saipan, Guam, Tinian, Pelelui, Angaur, Ulithi, Leyte, Luzon, Iwo Jama, Kerama Retto, Keisa Shima, Okinawa, Ia Shima, Minna Shima, Theya Shima, and Borneo.

41

UDT men underway in their LCPR launched from their Amphibious Personnel Destroyer (APD). They are in route to conduct a pre-assault reconnaissance and demolition operation. The date and location of the photograph are not known, but thought to be during the landings at South Kyasha, Japan.

On 17 June 1945, all UDTs were ordered to report to ATB Oceanside, California to begin cold-water training in preparation for the invasion of Japan. This included UDT-30, the last UDT to be established at Fort Pierce during the war, and the only standing UDT not to have completed advanced training at Maui. The men were to report no later than 15 August. However, before all the men could assemble, President Harry S. Truman ordered the use of atomic bombs at Hiroshima, Japan on 6 August and again at Nagasaki, Japan on 14 August, thus abruptly ending hostilities and the Japanese surrendered. The UDT men were then given a non-combat mission for the occupation of the Japanese Islands. Occupation reconnaissance and demolition duties were performed by numerous UDTs at Japan, Korea, and China.

It is a little-published fact that the Pacific UDT men were the most highly decorated Navy combatants of World War II. Collectively, they were awarded two Navy Cross Medals, 150 Silver Star Medals, 750 Bronze Star Medals, and numerous Purple Heart Medals. This was an astounding feat for men that carried no weapon other than a web belt with a military issue K-Bar knife.

WWII UDT-18 combat swimmers seen after completing their reconnaissance and demolition tasks at Balikpapan, Borneo on 1 July 1945. In this photograph, they are said to be watching Japanese kamikaze planes attacking U.S. Navy ships.

Including UDT-1 and UDT-2, a total of 30 UDTs were formed in the Pacific during WWII; each with an average of 100 officers and men. Only four 50-man teams survived during the postwar period. UDT-1 and UDT-3 were home-ported at ATB Coronado, CA and UDT-2 and UDT-4 were sent to ATB Little Creek, Norfolk, VA. The UDTs were organized doctrinally under the Amphibious Forces Pacific and Atlantic respectively. In 1983, some 38 years and two wars later, all UDTs were reorganized as SEAL Teams and still serve at these locations.

Office of Strategic Services Maritime Unit

Operational Swimmer Groups
One of the most influential, but little-known units from the World War II groups was the Joint-Service component of the Office of Strategic Services (OSS) Maritime Unit (MU). This secretive organization became the source of many postwar UDT capabilities. Indeed, the men of the Maritime Unit provided the early tactics, technology, and techniques still seen today in SEAL and SEAL Delivery Vehicle Teams and also NSW's Special Boat Teams.

The OSS Special Operations (SO) Branch established a Marine Section on 20 January 1943, with responsibilities for planning and conducting clandestine actions and activities from the sea. On 10 June, they were designated the Maritime Unit with branch status within the OSS hierarchy. MU was assigned responsibilities for planning and coordinating the clandestine infiltration of agents by sea, supplying resistance groups, engaging in maritime sabotage, and developing special equipment to accomplish maritime special operations.

GM3c Gordon Soltau, USN, Coxswain James Talmadge, USCG, and Coxswain Gene Ward, USCG deployed with the OSS Maritime Unit to Ceylon, India with Detachment 104. These men and other conducted many raids and reconnaissance operations in the China-India-Burma (CBI) Theater of Operations.

Combat diving was one key component, coupled with small-boat handling and training of commandos. Much of this training occurred south of Washington, DC in the vicinity of Doncaster, Maryland, a quiet and remote location on the Potomac River somewhat opposite the Marine Corps Base at Quantico, Virginia. Code named "Area D," it was originally Civilian Conservation Corps Camp S-43 during the depression, but was unused when the war broke out.

Royal Navy Commander Herbert G. A. Woolley, DSC (Distinguished Service Cross), established and directed the maritime group. He was on loan to OSS headquarters in Washington, DC, and was assisted by his officers LT Jack Taylor, USNR; 1st Lt. Frederic Wadley, AUS; Maj. Albert Lichtman, USMC; LT Robert Duncan, USNR and later by CPT Chris Lambertsen, MC, AUS, who became their primary medical doctor and trainer.

The Maritime Unit swimmers made good use of the swimming pool at the U.S. Naval Academy, where they began their diver training on 17 May 1943. Here, Dr. Lambertsen taught them diving physiology and the technical aspects of his new diving apparatus. For advanced training, the group was moved to Camp Pendleton, California and Catalina Island and subsequently to Nassau, Bahamas. The first generation of U.S. combat divers was soon accomplished in the tactics and techniques of clandestine maritime special operations with unique skills in underwater navigation and sabotage.

The first field group organized was the L-Unit, which was sent to England for operations in the European Theater of Operations (ETO).

Lambertsen Amphibious Respiratory Unit
In November 1942, Chris Lambertsen, then a University of Pennsylvania medical student, presented the concept of a self-contained diving apparatus to the Navy, which was built upon the concept of re-breathing pure oxygen after it had been filtered chemically. Once perfected, it was called the "Lambertsen Lung" and eventually the Lambertsen Amphibious Respiratory Unit or simply LARU.

The LARU would provide a well trained operative the capability to swim bubble-free underwater, and thus, to maneuver around target areas without detection from above. With development of this system, the U.S. Navy would be postured to take its place in the front ranks of countries with the ability to clandestinely employ underwater swimmers against an adversary. During this period, however, the Navy's only divers were in the salvage corps, and they were uninterested in the capability. OSS, however, saw the possibilities immediately.

Office of Strategic Services (OSS) Maritime Unit (MU) combat diver is training with the Lambertsen Amphibious Respiratory Unit (LARU) during WWII.

The OSS MU Swimmer Groups

The L-Unit was the first swimmer group to be deployed. This group went to England during the period 2 January through 22 June 1944. It was commanded by Captain Chadborne Gilpatric, AUS, and had at various times 17 officers and men. It was established with two subgroups: L-Unit #1 (initial cadre), led by Captain James B. Hodge, AUS and L-Unit #2 (supplemental cadre), led by Lieutenant Frederic J. Wadley, AUS. The enlisted men were a mix of U.S. Army, Navy, Coast Guard, and Marine Corps personnel.

The L-Units' primary focus was clandestine attacks along the Seine River in France to sabotage navigational aids and attack German submarines; however, they were never committed operationally. After the Allies established their beachhead in Normandy and the land battle began, the group was returned to the Bahamas, where they were re-designated Operational Swimmer Group #3 or OSG-3. Here they were retrained for deployment in the Pacific and in January1945 was assigned to OSS Detachment 101/104 in Ceylon, India, where they would join OSG-2 already deployed.

In June 1944, the 29 officers and men, who made up OSG-1 were loaned to the Navy for integration into UDT-10 at the Naval Combat Demolition Training and Experimental Base at Maui. UDT-10 was commanded by OSS-MU trained Navy Lieutenant Commander Arthur O. Choate, Jr. It was UDT-10 that introduced swim fins to the UDTs, and they were quickly adopted for obvious reasons.

UDT men on mess decks of USS Burrfish *before making their first nighttime reconnaissance at Pelilu; (l-r) Warren Christensen, Bill Moore, LT M.R. Massey, John MacMahon (KIA), and Leonard Barnhill.*

Once in Maui, five of the OSS trained UDT-10 men and one of the UDT instructors volunteered for a special nearshore reconnaissance mission schedule for August 1944. Transported by the submarine *USS Burrfish* (SS-312), the UDT men conducted clandestine reconnaissance around the islands of Peleliu and Gagil Tomil of the Yap Island Group. Over the course of the nights of August 17 and 18, three men were lost: QM1 Robert A. Black, Jr. and Sp(A)1c John C. MacMahon, USNR, were OSS trained, and CGM(M) Howard L. Roeder, who was a legendary UDT Chief Petty Officer. They were missing and presumed dead, however, it was discovered after the war that the Japanese captured and killed them. This historic mission was the first and only submarine-launched UDT operation of the war.

OSG-2 with 35 officers and men and OSG-3 with 25 officers and men, were assigned to the China-Burma-India (CBI) Theater of Operations and also allocated by OSS to prepare for the invasion of Japan. OSG-2 was commanded by Coast Guard Lieutenant Junior Grade John P. Booth. OSG-3, which had previously made up the L-Unit, remained split into two smaller groups,

Post-mission photo aboard USS Burrfish *at Pelilu: (l-r) CPO John Ball, John MacMahon (KIA), Bob Black (KIA), Emmet L. Carpenter, and CPO Howard Roeder (KIA).*

with Group One commanded by Army Captain J.J. Camp and Group Two commanded by Marine Corps Captain Richard E. Sullivan. Because of a wide range of disagreements with General Donovan, however, General MacArthur refused to allow OSS to operate under his command. This was apparently because he considered their methods too unconventional and unorthodox, which of course they were. MU men were subsequently assigned to OSS Detachment 101 and the South East Asia Command (SEAC) in Kandy, Ceylon, where they trained and operationally supported the British 14th Army along the coast of Burma as Detachment 404, primarily with landing party boat support.

Oddly, Japanese targets were declared out of bounds for the OSS swimmers. As a result, they conducted only one operation, the reconnaissance of Ramree Island off the western coast of Burma, in preparation for a landing by British troops. The stealthy tactics and techniques of OSS combat swimmers were not used in a direct action role against Japanese targets. Their capabilities, however, were not totally wasted. They had access to the British-designed submersible called "Sleeping Beauty," which they called a submersible canoe, to plan targets and practice tactics using this vessel for what they thought was the inevitable invasion of Japan. When Japan surrendered, the Maritime Unit was quickly disbanded along with whole of the OSS itself.

The British designed "submersible canoe" called Sleeping Beauty.

While the OSS has been the subject of numerous books and movies, the men of the Maritime Unit remained largely in the shadows until documents were released to the public in 1995.

"Father of U.S. Combat Diving"
The Lambertsen Legacy

University of Pennsylvania medical student Chris Lambertsen, inventor of the LARU, became a Captain in the Army Medical Corps during WWII and was tasked to become the OSS MU medical officer and primary trainer for diving operations. His foremost impact on UDT and subsequently SEAL capabilities came after the war.

After OSS was disbanded, and before being reassigned to hospital duty in Atlanta, Georgia after hostilities ended, Captain Lambertsen went to great lengths to save OSS MU's diving equipment, which included a large supply of LARUs. He began a passionate campaign to introduce LARU diving capabilities the U.S. Coast Guard, U.S. Army Engineers, and more importantly the U.S. Navy's Underwater Demolition Teams. This led to an interaction with the already infamous Navy Lieutenant Commander Douglas "Red Dog" Fane, who had overall command of the UDTs in the Atlantic in 1947.

With a kick start from Dr. Lambertsen personally, submarine and underwater swimmer trials were conducted aboard *USS Grouper* (SS-214) at St. Thomas, USVI in 1948. This resulted in UDTs fully adopting OSS capabilities, which the UDT men simply called "Submersible Operations" or SUBOPS. They immediately classified these capabilities to protect the clandestine tactics, techniques, and equipment being employed.

Dr. Lambertsen sent a letter to the Chief of Naval Operations on 17 June 1949 in which he outlined underwater swimmer capabilities and advocated their further development:

> *"The potential scope of trained UDT personnel is indicated by the following operational missions, which have been proven feasible by combined results of tests or wartime operations carried out by U.S. Navy Underwater Demolition Team, U.S. Office of Strategic Services, and by underwater swimmers of other nations including Italy, Germany, and England:*
>
> *1. Undetected day or night reconnaissance of enemy beaches, rivers, and harbors with photography where conditions permit.*
>
> *2. Undetected day or night underwater demolition of beach obstacles.*
>
> *3. Undetected day or night observation of enemy surface activities, with photography when conditions are favorable.*
>
> *4. Undetected night demolition attacks on enemy shipping and harbor installations such as docks and net defenses.*
>
> *Each of the several operational missions is predicated upon stealth. Ideally, each mission could be carried out using water as concealment during all phases. Practically, breaches of stealth are occasionally required. It is toward the goal of reducing*

to a minimum the breaches of stealth technique that the U.S. Navy Underwater Demolition Teams are now working."

This was a decisive period for the UDTs, since the LARU and OSS tactics, techniques, and procedures provided them a truly clandestine operational capability and vastly improved their maritime special operations potential. Capabilities introduced by Dr. Lambertsen also included use of the "Sleeping Beauty," a diver-transport vessel acquired from the British and called a submersible canoe. This would lead to decades of extensive UDT combatant submersible development and refinement. For the next three decades, the UDTs would experiment with Swimmer Propulsion Units (SPUs) or Swimmer Delivery Vehicles (SDVs), and a host of specially modified conventional and nuclear submarines dedicated to supporting maritime special operations. This culminated in 1983 with the organization and establishment of U.S. Navy SEAL Delivery Vehicle Teams.

USCG LT John Booth diving with the LARU during training and filming operations in Silver Spring, Florida.

Because the OSS was organized for such a brief period, and because their activities during and after the war remained so highly classified, the men of OSS MU received little or no recognition. Most of them returned from the war and simply faded back into society; never disclosing or discussing what they did. Numerous books and articles have been written about OSS activities, but very little about the Maritime Unit, whose capabilities were surreptitiously migrated into the UDTs and continue today with the SEAL teams.

Postwar Underwater Demolition Teams

Little has been written about the UDTs during the period between the wars, thus, there remains an unintended obscurity about their activities during the late 1940s. Only four 50-man UDTs were established after WWII. They included UDT-1 and UDT-3 at ATB Coronado, California, and UDT-2 and UDT-4 at ATB, Little Creek, Norfolk, Virginia—making them the first UDTs to be organized within the Atlantic Fleet.

The UDTs were the only naval commando units to survive doctrinally after WWII, and they were left with little manpower and even less operational and maintenance budgets. During this period and until Korea, the UDTs struggled simply to survive.

Lieutenant Commander Francis Douglas "Red Dog" Fane, innovative commander of the UDTs.

LCDR Francis Douglas "Red Dog" Fane stands out as the foremost and spectacular visionary who brought UDTs into the future. He had completed training at Fort Pierce late in the war and became commanding officer of UDT-13 during the occupation phase in Japan. After hostilities ended, he became commander of the UDTs within the Atlantic Amphibious Force. LCDR Fane did everything he could to keep UDT in the limelight. This included often unorthodox stunts, demonstrations, experimentations, and activities that created numerous newspaper and magazine articles. In 1947, LCDR Fane and Dr. Chris Lambertsen, who had been the primary trainer of combat swimmer tactics, techniques, and procedures with OSS MU during WWII, collaborated on the same training for the UDT men. Dr. Lambertsen was the inventor of the Lambertsen Amphibious Respiratory Unit or LARU, which was employed by OSS during war and adopted by the UDTs under LCDR Fane.

Together with Dr. Lambertsen, they took the UDTs underwater to develop a completely new capability surrounding "Submersible Operations" or SUBOPS as it would be generally characterized by the men. This included the first series of submarine lock-out and lock-in operations; including operations with the "Sleeping Beauty." This period emphasized the need for focused research and experimentation. It was also a decisive period for the UDTs, since the OSS tactics and techniques provided the UDT men a truly clandestine combat diving capability. Expanding the scope of their capabilities also meant learning how to conduct submerged day or night reconnaissance of enemy beaches, attacking port and harbor facilities and ships, and intelligence collection of enemy activities without being detected. These new tactics and techniques also created demand for advances in technologies related to swimming and diving equipment, improved oxygen diving tables, explosives, demolition devices, diver communication equipment, and combatant submersibles; a practice of deliberate innovation that remains a proactive part of the SEAL teams today.

UDT men conducting experimental operations with Navy helicopters, circa 1948.

During 1947, too, LCDR Fane had UDT men experimenting with helicopters; however, during this period helicopters didn't have the space and lift capacity with which to develop any kind of operational capability. Moreover, helicopters were also not used by the UDT tactically during the Korean War period, and didn't actually become operationally tactical assets within Naval Special Warfare until employed by the SEAL teams and others during Vietnam.

Chapter 2:
Korea and the 1950s

The division of Korea was the result of the 1945 Allied victory in World War II, ending Japan's 35-year colonial rule of Korea. In a trusteeship, the U.S. and the Soviet Union agreed to temporarily occupy the country, establishing zones of control north and south of the 38th parallel. The purpose of the trusteeship was to establish a Korean provisional government for the entire country. Elections were scheduled, however, the Soviet Union refused to cooperate with United Nations plans to hold general and free elections in the two Korean zones. As a result, a Communist state was permanently established under Soviet auspices in the north and a pro-Western state was set up in the south. Two states were effectively established, and both claimed sovereignty over the entire Korean peninsula.

The U.S. honored its agreement and pulled out in September 1949, however, the Soviets spent the intervening years arming the North. With the Americans gone, Soviet leader Joseph Stalin supported North Korean leaders request to invade the south. American intelligence elements warned of an imminent attack, but the warnings were ignored. On 23 June 1950, U.N. observers inspected the border area and saw nothing amiss. In a stunning surprise just two days later, on the 25 June, the full force of the Korean People's Army (KPA) crossed the 38th parallel and declared war on South Korea. On 27 June, the U.N. Security Council authorized use of force to defend South Korea. Led by the U.S., the communist attack in Korea resulted in a quick buildup, and within a year, America had 3.3 million troops under arms.

UDT-3 LTjg George Atcheson was in Japan leading a 10-man detachment when war was declared. The UDT men were in Japan making beach surveys and working with U.S. Marines to train U.S. Army regimental combat teams in various amphibious reconnaissance techniques. LTjg Atcheson and his men left for Korea immediately.

———————————⟨⛤

First Combat Operation

Under cover of darkness on the night of 5 August 1950, this small detachment of UDT men infiltrated the Korean shoreline from the destroyer *USS Diachenko* (APD-123) aboard their inflatable boats. Their objective was to destroy a railroad bridge and tunnel under North Korean control near the port city of Yeosu.

BM3 Warren "Fins" Foley accompanied LTjg Atcheson as they swam through the swift current some 200 yards ahead of their boats as swimmer scouts. They climbed up a 35-foot seawall just below the target and conducted a quick reconnaissance. Seeing no one, they signaled the remainder of the team to bring the explosives ashore. Without warning, 10 North Korean soldiers came out of the tunnel on a hand car and opened fire on the team. Foley was wounded in the ensuing gun fight and tumbled over the seawall. LTjg Atcheson lobbed hand grenades at the North Koreans; giving him and his men time for recovery and return to the *Diachenko*. Foley ended up with a smashed kneecap and bullet wounds in his hand and thigh. He was the first Navy casualty of the Korean War.

———————————⟨⛤

Expanding Capabilities

During the month of August 1950, additional UDT personnel began to arrive, and were committed to the continuation of an expanding new mission involving nighttime coastal demolition raids against railroad tunnels and bridges. The UDT men were given the task because, in the words of UDT Lieutenant Ted Fielding, "We were ready to do what nobody else could do, and what nobody else wanted to do."

As a result, the Korean War became a pivotal time in UDT history, since it presented a stage for demonstrating their versatility and adaptability; where operations proved to be a catalyst for vastly increasing UDT tactics, techniques, and procedures; pointing to the need for improved and expanded operational capabilities throughout the war.

UDT operators clad in thermal protective "dry suits" are being briefed before a mission in the cold waters of Korea.

If only temporary, traditional UDT doctrinal roles were greatly expanded. In addition to amphibious reconnaissance and obstacle clearance, the scope of the UDT mission now included clandestine infiltrations from the sea for the purpose of conducting raids and attacking enemy shipping and port and harbor facilities, intelligence gathering and documentation, ordnance disposal, providing cover for withdrawing friendly forces, and rescuing downed airmen. The UDT men worked at sea and on land with CIA personnel, U.S. Marine Reconnaissance personnel, Royal Marine Commandos, and naval commandos from South Korea.

UDT men receiving a pre-mission briefing aboard ship during the Korean War.

Individual weaponry taken by the UDT men behind enemy lines was usually limited to the submachine guns, pistols, and knives, which they found most useful for the close-quarters combat that characterized most raiding missions. Though presumably available, sound suppressors for the weapons are not known to have been used. The men used a variety of demolitions in their work, but the standard UDT charge was the Mark-135 Demolition Pack, which contained twenty pounds of C-3 plastic explosive.

Accelerated Operational Tempo

The operational tempo for the UDT in the combat zone began to expand throughout the remainder of 1950. Deployment cycles began placing detachments of 30 men forward; generally aboard an Amphibious Personnel Destroyers (APD) for periods of six to eight weeks. Each detachment typically conducted 10 and 20 demolition or beach reconnaissance missions per embarkation; driven by enemy activity and contingent on the weather. In addition to these raids,

UDT personnel were frequently assigned temporary advisory and training duty with other military units or with CIA elements. Small teams were sometimes forward based on islands close to the coast of North Korea, standing alert duty with UN escape and evasion organizations to assist in the recovery of downed airmen.

Turning the Tide of War

UDT operators played a crucial early role in Operation CHROMITE on 15 September 1950 with the surprise amphibious assault on the city of Incheon. Men from UDT-1 and UDT-3 infiltrated ahead of the main landing to scout the mudflats, mark channels, and search for mines. During the assault, they worked to clear fouled propellers and keep channels clear. They remained after the assault to clear the harbor of unexploded mines, sunken or damaged vessels, and to put navigational aids in place. The Battle of Incheon marked the first defeat of the North Koreans and also resulted in the recapture of Seoul, the capital of South Korea.

Briefing of UDT members at Wonsan in October, 1950.

The next month, the UDT men were in Wonsan Harbor to help support mine clearing operation. Two U.S. minesweepers, the *USS Pirate* (AM-275) and *USS Pledge* (AM-277) hit mines and sank. UDT men assisted in the rescue of more than two dozen sailors from the water.

Later the next day, UDT operator William Giannotti, using an aqua lung, dove into Wonsan Harbor to locate and mark the wreck of the *Pledge* for Navy salvage divers with surface-supplied air, who would then destroy classified documents on the vessel. The operation marked the first combat dive by a UDT operator.

UDT men destroy facilities and abandoned United Nations supplies in Hungnam on 24 December 1950. The U.S. Navy Amphibious Personnel Destroyer USS Begore *(ADP-127) is in the foreground*

On Christmas Eve 1950, eight men from UDT-3 set off over 20 tons of explosives to destroy waterfront port facilities at Hungnam, Korea, which was being quickly overrun. The U.S. did not want the United Nations supplies abandoned at the harbor to be used by the North Koreans. UDT men worked for hours in biting cold, driving rain, and sniper fire. Their support ship *USS Begor* (APD-127) fended off Chinese soldiers with its 5-inch guns. Once the demolitions were emplaced, the UDT men started their timers and returned to the ship. The demolition shot went off as planned, resulting in the largest single blast of the Korean War and the largest non-nuclear explosion since WWII.

The goal of Operation FISHNET in September 1952 was to destroy North Korea's fishing industry, which was nearly as important to the economy as rice. By reducing their food supply, the UN allies hoped to put pressure on the North Korean government. UDT divers used their underwater skills to sabotage fishing nets. It was their last extensive operation of the war before the armistice of 27 July 1953, which ended fighting.

Expanding the Teams

Within the first six months of the war, half the Navy's entire UDT force was committed to the conflict, without knowing what direction this new war would take or how long it could last. UDT-1 and UDT-3 were rotating deployments during the early stages of the war, but, as the war progressed, it was clear that they needed further support. As a result, UDT-5 was established in September 1951 at Coronado to provide the badly needed support.

UDT-2 and UDT-4 in the Atlantic Amphibious Force were considered for Korea, however, they remained focused on experimental programs involving the Aqua Lung® development, lock-out and lock-in diving operations from submerged submarines, cold-weather diving operations, parachute training, and development and testing of miniature submarines and combatant submersibles.

Back to Business as Usual--World 1950s

The dramatic successes in Korea did little to change the status of the UDTs after the armistice. Navy leadership clung to a World War II mission profile despite Cold War realities and emerging new kinds of threats.

After the Korean armistice, the remainder of the 1950s was a relatively calm and somewhat lethargic period for the UDTs. During this period, the UDT men honed diving and submarine operational skills, began attending U.S. Army Airborne Schools, developed water-entry parachuting techniques, and experimented extensively with a host of swimmer propulsion units and swimmer delivery vehicles.

Operationally, UDT platoons made routine deployments with the Amphibious Forces to the Western Pacific, Atlantic and Caribbean, and Mediterranean areas, where they conducted numerous training events and amphibious training exercises.

UDT-21 officer Chris Bent and his men preparing to dive the Emerson pure oxygen rebreather.

Each UDT had an authorized manning of 15 line officers and 100 enlisted men. All were volunteers, who had to successfully completed UDT Basic Training, which was recognized as the most arduous training in the U. S. military. Each team was organized into operational platoons, which were supported by a headquarters staff. Except for some members of the headquarters staff, all of the officers and men were qualified UDT swimmers. The four operational platoons were capable of being deployed either independently, in combination, or as part of the entire team. When one or more platoons were deployed apart from the command, the senior line officer was designated the officer-in-charge.

Administratively, all officers and men were also assigned to one of the departments: Executive (commanding and executive officer), Operations, Supply, Engineering, Air Operations, Submersible Operations, Ordnance, 1st Lieutenant, and Medical. The headquarters element was also deployable, but as a general rule it would be split between the operating platoons if the team as a whole were to be deployed for combat operations.

UDT men preparing for diving operations while on deployment in the Mediterranean, circa 1958.

Each operating platoon had a compliment of two officers and 20 men, including one chief and one leading first class petty officer. The headquarters element was composed of the remaining officers, who were department heads, and at least one chief or senior petty officer in each department, who provided the necessary basic and advanced training to the operating platoons, which also had personnel with expertise from each department.

"New Look" Armed Forces

In the late 1950s, there was a growing and recognized need for military forces with special operations capabilities. This included the Army Special Forces or "Green Berets," Marines Corps Force Reconnaissance Units, and the Navy's Underwater Demolition Teams. During his final years in office, President Eisenhower began to proactively engage these specialized forces in places like Laos and Cuba.

Men of UDT-21 during Mediterranean deployment.

Few conventional thinkers believed that brushfire wars like Cuba and terrorism would dominate the world scene. Historically, special operations units in most nations had been created to conduct specific missions that conventional forces were either incapable of performing or saw no merit in performing. As a result, and with few exceptions, such special units were rarely recognized for their contributions and, more often than not, disbanded and allowed to fade into obscurity. Moreover, special mission units, by their very nature, conduct covert, clandestine, and other highly sensitive operations, which necessarily place their activities, both past and present, in a cloak of secrecy and generally at odds with conventional thinkers and planners.

UDT combat swimmer recovering aboard U.S. Navy Sikorsky H-34 "Seahorse" helicopter during training, circa 1958.

Chapter 3:
Birth of the SEALs

Admiral Arleigh Burke's Vision

The action and activities that would result in the establishment of U.S. Navy SEAL Teams actually began as early as 1958, when Admiral Arleigh A. Burke proposed the concept of covert military activities to keep the Communist powers off balance.

Admiral Burke, who had become the Chief of Naval Operations (CNO) in 1956, championed the cause to devote greater resources to the conduct of limited war. He argued that in an era of nuclear parity, paramount U.S. objectives should be deterrence of general war and the simultaneous maintenance of American global interests. He believed that for the Soviet Union, the fulcrum of struggle would surround the underdeveloped regions of the free world.

In early 1960, Admiral Burke directed the Navy staff to explore organizing new or existing Navy and Marine Corps units for smaller conflicts. He directed his staff to study the Navy's options with respect to unconventional warfare. After some period, the staff concluded: "...that the Underwater Demolition Teams and USMC reconnaissance units are organizations capable of expansion into unconventional warfare." An Unconventional Activities Working Group was formally established the following September to investigate "naval unconventional activity methods, techniques and concepts, which may be employed effectively against Sino-Soviet interests under conditions of cold war."

It is very likely that the failed Bay of Pigs operation resulted in detailed discussions and decision opportunities between President Kennedy and the National Security team, and encouragement of the military services to accelerate activities involving the capabilities of their special mission units.

The concept for development of an improved "Naval Guerrilla/ Counter-Guerrilla Warfare" capability within the U.S. Navy and first-time mention of "SEAL" units was the subject of a 10 March 1961 Memorandum to Admiral Burke from his staff that provided recommendations for review, validation, and approval. Operations conducted in "restricted waters" was emphasized: "One unit each is proposed under the Pacific and Atlantic amphibious commanders, and will represent a center or focal point through which all elements of this specialized Navy capability (naval guerrilla warfare) would be channeled." The same memorandum stated that, "An appropriate name for such units could be 'SEAL' units; SEAL being a contraction of SEA, AIR, LAND, and thereby, indicating an all-around, universal capability."

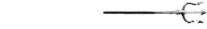

Sea-Air-Land Teams

For reasons still difficult to understand, it has often been declared that President John F. Kennedy personally directed formation of the SEAL Teams, but this is entirely wrong. The Navy staff had been working on the problem of Unconventional Warfare long before President Kennedy took office, however, the president did tacitly recognize the need in a speech on 25 May 1961 before a special joint session of Congress. In this address he stated that, "I am directing the Secretary of Defense to expand rapidly and substantially, in cooperation with our Allies, the orientation of existing forces for the conduct of non-nuclear war, paramilitary operations and sub limited or unconventional wars. In addition, our special forces and unconventional warfare units will be increased and reoriented." That statement is as close as President Kennedy ever got toward personally directing establishment of SEAL Teams.

President John F. Kennedy inspects members of SEAL Team TWO during a visit to the Naval Amphibious Base, Little Creek, Norfolk, Virginia.

After considerable study, it was determined by the Navy staff that expanding the UDT mission would likely inhibit their doctrinal Amphibious Force mission and responsibilities. It was, therefore, concluded that new Unconventional Warfare operational units should be established. Also, that these new units should embrace the characteristics of the UDTs, but incorporate new capabilities like those developed and practiced during the Korean War. Moreover, the UDTs had been doctrinally tied to Amphibious Force since WWII and, as a result, they had been denied opportunities to utilize U.S. Army and Marine Corps training schools, nor had they been given funding or authorizations to purchase the kinds of equipment needed for expanded missions involving operations from the sea, air, or land. It was intended, thus, that these new SEAL units would not be doctrinally hindered and given freedom to establish a broader and more flexible mission.

In a letter dated 11 December 1961, the CNO officially authorized establishment of one SEAL Team in the Atlantic and Pacific Fleets with an effective date of 1 January 1962. This letter resulted in the authority and funding to officially establish SEAL

Team ONE and TWO; after almost four years of investigation, it resulted in what Admiral Burke had envisioned—an Unconventional Warfare capability within the Navy.

Both new SEAL Teams would be formed with men already assigned to UDT-11, UDT-12 and UDT-21. In a parallel path, the reestablishment of UDT-22 in the Atlantic had also been authorized for 1 February 1962, however, because of lack of manpower and funding, this team was not organized until the following August.

Cuban Operations
In the late 1950s Cuba was a communist state ruled by the dictator Fidel Castro. Little has been told about UDT and SEAL Team experiences during this historic Cuban period, however, UDT men participated in activities preparatory to the Bay of Pigs operation initiated in April 1961, and detachments from UDT-21 and SEAL Teams ONE and TWO were deployed for operations during the Cuban Missile Crisis in October 1962. Members of the Little Creek-based SEALs were also engaged in actions and activities surrounding Operation MONGOOSE from 1962 to 1965, which involved a CIA operation designed to overthrow Fidel Castro and his regime.

Bay of Pigs
In April 1960, the CIA began recruiting anti-Castro Cuban exiles in the Miami, Florida area. Between April and July 1960, assessment and training was carried out on the barrier islands of Florida and at various other facilities in South Florida, such as Miami and Homestead Air Force Base, where a series of "safe houses" had been established. UDT personnel trained 12 hand-selected Cuban exiles in advanced swimming and demolition training at the southern part of Vieques Island, Puerto Rico. These exiles were later moved to an abandoned U.S. Army training base situated south of New Orleans, Louisiana, where the operatives did pool work, trained in rudimentary patrolling, small-boat handling, and maritime infiltration tactics and techniques. They were eventually sent to Puerto Cabezas, Nicaragua to join the larger invasion force.

On the night of 17 April 1961, two landing craft with a CIA "operations officer" and five U.S. trained Cuban frogmen entered the Bay of Pigs (Bahía de Cochinos) on the southern coast of Cuba. American UDT men aboard the *USS Chopper* (SS-342) at Mayport, FL, and were reportedly inserted near Havana to conduct harbor and beach reconnaissance; although it has never been acknowledged that any U.S. personnel went ashore.

Cuban Missile Crisis

In October 1962 a 13-day confrontation began between the United States and the Soviet Union, which had begun building missile-launching facilities in Cuba. This confrontation is often regarded by historians as the closest incident of the Cold War that could have resulted in a nuclear exchange between the U.S. and the Soviet Union.

After the U.S. had placed nuclear missiles aimed at the Soviet Union at strategic locations in Turkey and Italy, President Nikita Khrushchev in turn proposed the placement of missiles in Cuba, which could be aimed at the U.S. A secret meeting between Khrushchev and Fidel Castro in July 1962 resulted in the construction of several missile sites in Cuba, which began almost immediately that summer.

These activities were quickly detected by U-2 spy aircraft, which had obtained undisputable photographic evidence of medium- and intermediate-range nuclear missiles being placed in Cuba. The U.S. demanded the dismantling of the missiles sites, and considered many options, including assaulting Cuba from the air and sea, but decided instead upon a "quarantine" or military blockade of ships and aircraft entering Cuba.

Detachments from UDT-21 and SEAL Teams ONE and TWO were dispatched as part of the military buildup in the event that a full-scale invasion of Cuba was warranted. Most of the men were sent to the Naval Station at Key West, Florida, where they embarked submarines for intelligence planning and training and rehearsals for designated reconnaissance or direct action operations in Cuba.

Operation MONGOOSE

Operation MONGOOSE was a multi-year CIA activity conducted between late 1962 through 1965. It involved a highly secret operational plan for the overthrow of Fidel Castro and the

70

Communist regime in Cuba. The operational plan involved insurgent operations to be performed by Cubans from within Cuba—with outside help from the U.S. and elsewhere. SEAL personnel assigned to the CIA participated in much of the "unconventional" planning and worked directly with the CIA to establish and operate a series of "safe houses" in and around the Miami, Florida. SEAL personnel trained Cuban commando teams in small boat operations, beach reconnaissance, and combat swimmer methods. Much of this training was accomplished at non-descript locations that were positioned in and around the Florida Keys.

SEAL Developments

Through their operations, actions, and activities, SEALs began to establish what would become an exceptional record of accomplishment in Vietnam. At the time of their formation and throughout much of the Vietnam conflict, the existence of the SEAL Teams was highly guarded outside of the military. When the SEAL Teams were formed in January 1962, there was only one team each in the Atlantic and Pacific Fleets. Both teams were commanded by a Navy Lieutenant with a complement of 10 officers and 50 men, and they actually remained this size until a buildup occurred with the rest of the navy in Vietnam during the mid to late 1960s. Regardless their operational success, the SEALs struggled to survive drastic downsizing after Vietnam, since there was no doctrinal place for them in the U.S. Navy. It is difficult to comprehend today, but terms like special operations, special naval operations, and naval special warfare were not commonly used in military circles, and especially within the Navy. Moreover, there were only a few in the Navy who fully understood their meaning, and those that did were largely the men in the UDT and SEAL Teams, who reverently referred to themselves as the "Naval Special Warfare community," which has become, and remains, extremely strong and cohesive.

Naval Operations Support Groups

Naval Operations Support Group (NOSG) staffs were established in November 1963 to support the SEALs, UDTs, Beach

Jumper Units (BJUs), and Boat Support Units (BSUs). One staff each in the Atlantic and Pacific was established for collaborative planning among the combined units. These NOSGs were the forerunners of the Naval Special Warfare Groups that remain today. The name was changed in 1967, when they were called Naval Special Warfare Groups Atlantic and Pacific.

Two BJUs were an odd addition to the NOSGs. They were special-mission cover and deception units organized during World War II, but, like many other special units, were eliminated at war's end. They were established again for Korea with an expanded fleet mission, and during Vietnam accomplished operations more along the lines of Psychological Warfare. In the early 1970s, the BJUs were divested from their Unconventional Warfare mission and returned to the Fleet Commanders. Also in the early 1970s the Naval Special Warfare Groups were eliminated and absorbed into the Naval Inshore Warfare (NIW) Commands, supporting the Amphibious Forces Atlantic and Pacific. The NIWs were Major Navy Commands led by a two-star admiral. The command's organizational structure was a completely mis-led disaster and, as a result, it only lasted a couple of years, when the Naval Special Warfare Groups were reestablished as NSWG-1 and NSWG-2.

Boat Support Units

The BSUs were a new concept, and the SEALs might not have been as successful as they were in Vietnam without their support. BSU-1 in Coronado, California sent specially trained Mobile Support Teams (MST) to Vietnam, where they supported SEAL platoons working throughout the Delta Rivers and canals of South Vietnam. These units were made up of fleet personnel especially trained to provide dedicated maritime mobility and boat maintenance. Although other units supported SEALs during the Vietnam period, only the BSUs and the West Coast-organized MSTs were specifically established to support SEALs. The BSU men created the pathway and growth that resulted in the Special Boat Teams that are such an integral part of NSW today, and the Special Warfare Combatant-craft Crewmen or SWCC warfare-area specialty. The men now have their own Navy rating: Special Boat Operator and their own distinguishing breast insignia.

SEALs in Vietnam

Shortly after being established in January 1962, SEAL Team ONE deployed Chief Petty Officers Robert Sullivan and Charles Raymond to take initial surveys and make preparations for training South Vietnamese naval personnel in the tactics, techniques and procedures of maritime special operations. Later, SEAL detachments of varying size were initially deployed to Vietnam in and around DaNang, where they trained South Vietnamese commandos in guerrilla and anti-guerrilla tactics, diving, demolitions, and hand-to-hand combat.

In April 1962 LTjg Philip P. Holts and LTjg Jon R. Stockholm of SEAL Team ONE (ST-1) led a combined ST-1 and SEAL Team TWO (ST-2) nine-man advisory detachment to Vietnam. Their mission was to train selected Vietnamese Coastal Force personnel in reconnaissance, sabotage, and guerrilla warfare and, to prepare them to instruct succeeding classes of Biet Hai commandos. In the photo standing (l-r) are SF1 Robert F. Fisher (ST-1), FTG2 Carl D. Marriott (ST-1), SN Robert D. Paul (ST-1), and SK2 William E. Burbank (ST-2). Kneeling: SM2 David A. Wilson (ST-1), DM2 Alwyn J. Smith, Jr. (ST-1), DM1 Lenard A. Waugh (ST-2), and EN2 Theodore E George (ST-1). Not in the photograph was BM1 Jack R. Perkins (ST-1).

During this period, the U.S. Government agreed to increase aid to South Vietnam in the fight against Viet Cong (properly the Viet Nam Cong San or Vietnamese Communists) rebels and their North Vietnamese supporters. The agreement included paying for a larger Vietnamese army and navy, and placing more U.S. advisors into the field. Viet Cong, or VC as they were commonly known, was a term applied to about 10,000 troops that remained in South Vietnam after the end of the First Indochina War (1946-1954). The VC at first used subversive tactics to overthrow the South Vietnamese regime, but later resorted to open warfare. They were subsequently reinforced by large numbers of North Vietnamese troops infiltrating into the south.

Navy SEAL Frank Thornton seen in his advisory role with South Vietnamese Provincial Reconnaissance Unit (PRU) commandos. SEAL operators performed numerous advise and assist missions in Vietnam.

As the war continued, SEAL Team ONE platoons were positioned in the Rung Sat Special Zone, where they began disrupting VC troop and supply movements. Later they progressed much further into the Mekong Delta to accomplish expanded river and inland waterway operations. SEAL Team TWO platoons and advisors would eventually be deployed to Vietnam to relieve the pressure on SEAL Team ONE and allow for expanded operations. Platoons from SEAL Team ONE and TWO were assigned to specific operational areas in Vietnam and for the most part operated almost autonomously.

While the vast majority of SEAL operations were conducted after inserting from boats, it was in Vietnam that SEALs first began developing hit-and-run operations using U.S. Army and Navy helicopters. These operations involved Huey helicopters in "slick" or passenger configurations, but they were also lightly armed with door guns. SEALs also operated closely and routinely with the U.S. Navy's Helicopter Attack Squadron (Light) Three (HAL-3) detachments. Known as Seawolves, they were often co-located with SEALs and provided extensive rocket and gunfire support. "Scramble Seawolves!" was the radio call made when SEALs needed immediate assistance. Seawolves flew UH-1B Huey gunships in all weather, day or night, to provide close-air support, medical evacuation, and insertion and extraction of SEAL squads during many missions conducted at night and in inclement weather.

SEAL Team ONE platoon in Vietnam. This photograph displays the typical look of SEALs prepared to go on a mission in the Delta region of Vietnam.

SEAL platoons carried out day and night ambushes–with a strong preference for night operations, hit-and-run raids and ambushes, reconnaissance patrols, and special intelligence collection operations.

A Seawolf UH-1B firing rockets.

SEALs and the Phoenix Program

SEALs were involved in Operation Phoenix, which was a classified military, intelligence, and internal security coordination program designed by the CIA during the Vietnam War. It was largely functional between 1967 and 1972. The program was designed to identify and "neutralize"—via capture-kill and infiltration—and intended to disrupt the civilian Viet Cong Infrastructure (VCI). The VCI collected taxes and provided political direction and control of North Vietnam's war within the villages and hamlets throughout South Vietnam.

SEALs and Covert Maritime Operations

A Maritime Operations Group called OP 37 was organized under the code name Naval Advisory Detachment (NAD) in Da Nang, Vietnam. OP 37 was a highly-classified U.S. program of covert actions against North Vietnam; consisting of agent team insertions, reconnaissance missions, and naval sabotage operations. It was started in 1961 by the CIA. In 1964 the program was transferred to the Military Assistance Command, Vietnam Studies and Observations Group (MACSOG), which was a cover name for a Joint Unconventional Warfare Task Force (JUTWF). SEAL and NSW Mobile Support Teams (MSTs) provided training and assistance, but were officially restricted from participating in actual missions.

Chapter 4:
Evolving through the 1970s and 1980s

SEALs in Grenada–Operation URGENT FURY

On 25 October 1983, tensions between the U.S. and the tiny island nation of Grenada caused the U.S. to invade the island to ensure the safety of the U.S. citizens living there. SEAL Teams were attached to the U.S. forces to aid in the assault, and this would be their first introduction to declared combat since Vietnam.

One SEAL element was kept busy conducting beach and back shore reconnaissance for U.S. Marines coming ashore at Pearls Airfield on the eastern shore. Two days later the same SEALs were relocated to the west side of the island, where they performed three additional beach recons.

Other SEALs were focused on the extraction of Grenada's Governor-General and the capture of Grenada's only radio tower. Because of a lack of current intelligence, neither mission was well briefed or sufficiently supported, causing the SEALs many difficulties from the very beginning. Foremost was the delay in an airborne transport that caused their daytime calm-sea insertion to be pushed back to night time and bad storm conditions. One of their two transport planes missed its drop zone, and four SEALs were lost in a rain-squall off the island's coast. Their bodies were never recovered. The remaining SEALs split into two groups and proceeded to their objectives at the radio tower and Governor's mansion.

While setting up at the Governor's mansion, the men realized that their satellite communications equipment was still on their insertion helicopter. As Grenadian and Cuban troops began moving in, the SEAL's only radio ran out of battery power. They were forced to improvise and used the mansion's landline telephone to direct AC-130 aircraft fire against the approaching enemy. The SEALs maintained position in the mansion overnight and moved out the following morning, when they were replaced by Force Reconnaissance Marines.

SEALs attacking the radio station also ran into communication problems, and were unable to raise their command group. After beating back several waves of Grenadian and Cuban troops, the SEALs decided their position too untenable. They destroyed the station and fought their way to the water, swam toward the open sea, and were picked up several hours later after being spotted by a reconnaissance plane.

Despite the difficulties encountered, the SEALs performed exceptionally during pre-assault reconnaissance operations, and were responsible for the rescue and evacuation of Governor Sir Paul Scoon. Operation URGENT FURY, for the most part, highlighted failures in planning, leadership, and communications; however, they were failures from which the SEALs could apply many lessons learned.

SEALs lost in Grenada were exceptional warriors. They were: Machinist Mate 1st Class Kenneth J. Butcher, Quartermaster 1st Class Kevin E. Lundberg, Hull Technician 1st Class Stephen L. Morris, and Senior Chief Engineman Robert R. Schamberger. They were the first SEALs lost in combat operations since Vietnam.

SEALs and the *Achille Lauro* Mission

The *MS Achille Lauro* was a cruise ship based in Naples, Italy. On 7 October 1985, four heavily armed Palestinian terrorists hijacked the ship in the Mediterranean Sea off the coast of Alexandria, Egypt. Some 320 crewmembers and 80 passengers were taken hostage. Identifying themselves as members of the Palestine Liberation Front—a Palestinian splinter group—the gunmen demanded the release of 50 Palestinian militants imprisoned in Israel. If their demands were not met, they threatened to blow up the ship and kill the 11 Americans on board. The next morning, they also threatened to kill the British passengers. At this juncture, highly trained U.S. Navy SEAL assault forces were launched from the U.S. to capture or kill the terrorists before they could harm any of the *Achille Lauro's* passengers or crew.

The *Achille Lauro* traveled to the Syrian port of Tartus, where the terrorists demanded negotiations on 8 October. Syria refused to permit the ship to anchor in its waters, which prompted more threats from the hijackers. That afternoon, they shot and killed Leon Klinghoffer, a 69-year-old Jewish-American, who was confined to a wheelchair as the result of a stroke. His body was then pushed overboard in the wheelchair. The ship then headed back toward Port Said, where, after two days of negotiations, the hijackers agreed to abandon the ship and surrendered to the Egyptians in exchange for safe passage to Tunisia.

On 10 October, the four hijackers boarded an Egypt Air Boeing 737 airliner, which took off from Cairo and headed for Tunisia. U.S. Navy carrier based F-14 "Tomcat" fighters located the airliner 80 miles south of Crete and, without announcing themselves, trailed the airliner in darkness. After requests to land at Tunis and Athens airports were refused, the F-14s turned on their running lights, flew wing-to-wing with the airliner, and ordered it to land at the Naval Air Station and NATO base in Sigonella, Sicily.

Unbeknownst to the terrorists, the U.S. Navy SEAL assault force was also trailing behind them in two U.S. Air Force C-141 transport aircraft. When all aircraft landed somewhat simultaneously at Sigonella, the SEAL assault force immediately surrounded the escape plane with all intentions of capturing the terrorists and taking them into custody.

Simultaneously, however, Italian Prime Minister Bettino Craxi claimed Italian territorial rights over the NATO base, and deployed Italian Air Force personnel and Carabinieri (the national military police of Italy), who lined up surrounding the SEALs. A delicate international standoff ensued, but the situation was resolved before an assault became necessary. The U.S. eventually capitulated to the Italians and allowed the hijackers to be taken into Italian custody after receiving assurances that the hijackers would be tried for murder.

On 10 July 1986, an Italian court convicted three of the terrorists and sentenced them to prison terms ranging from 15 to 30 years. The fourth hijacker was a minor who was tried and convicted separately.

―――――――――⟨⟨

SEALs in Panama – Operation JUST CAUSE

On 20 December 1989, the United States invaded the country of Panama during Operation JUST CAUSE, where U.S. Navy SEALs were tasked to disable a private boat and an airplane that General Manuel Noriega, the president of Panama, might use to escape his country. The boat attack was a classic combat swimmer operation, where SEALs, equipped with pure-oxygen diving apparatus, swam undetected underwater for some distance and successfully placed explosives under the target vessel. It was "disabled" with enough explosives under the hull that one engine was never found.

The airfield operation was successful, but not without complications. Noriega's airplane was destroyed; however, four SEALs were killed during the operation and eight seriously wounded. The failure of this mission started during the planning process, which called for 48 SEALs in two strike-force elements to be inserted near cliffs at the end of the runway. The SEALs would then patrol along the 3,500-foot long airfield to the hangar, where General Noriega's Learjet was kept. One group would disable the airplane, while others would provide security and pull small airplanes onto the airstrip to block its use.

H-hour (the time the attack was to begin) was set for 0100 on 19 December 1989. At 0045, the SEAL commander was notified that H-hour had been moved forward 15 minutes, because fighting had already broken out between Panamanian and American forces. As the SEALs continued toward their objective, however, several problems began to occur.

The USAF Combat Controller attached to the SEALs had not been able to raise the Air Force Special Operations Command AC-130 aircraft assigned to provide supporting fire if needed. This was important because, when the SEALs infiltrated, there would be no cover for concealment. Additionally, they discovered that the runway was well lit by landing lights and backscatter from the city. Also, a fire from the nearby city began waking up house guards in buildings surrounding the field.

One group of SEALs established a position about 100 feet from the hangar, another slightly behind and to the side of the first. A call came out from the hangar for the SEALs to surrender, and they responded by demanding the Panamanians surrender. At that point, several long bursts of gunfire came out from the hangar, and house guards from across the airfield also began firing; putting the SEALs in a deadly crossfire. In the initial volley, several SEALs were killed or wounded. Other SEALs began a barrage of fires to provide some element of protective cover. At this juncture, the Combat Controllers were able to establish contact with the C-130 gunship; however, they were too far away to provide immediate assistance.

Operation JUST CAUSE in Panama, where SEALs disabled President Noriega's private jet to prevent his escape from the country.

Surviving SEALs began dragging casualties to safety, and when so doing, others became casualties themselves. The Learjet was then ordered to be destroyed with the AT-4 (anti-tank weapon), which hit the aircraft cleanly, making it inoperable. The SEALs eventually maneuvered to safety and called for medical evacuation helicopters to remove the dead and wounded. The operation was clearly a tactical success; however, killed during the actions were Lieutenant John Connors, Chief Petty Officer Donald McFaul, Torpedoman's Mate 2nd Class Isaac Rodriguez, and Botswain's Mate 1st Class Chris Tilghman. Eight other SEALs were seriously wounded.

————————⊂⇥

DESERT STORM—SEALs in the Persian Gulf

The first major foreign crisis for the United States after the end of the Cold War presented itself in August 1990. Saddam Hussein, the dictator of Iraq, ordered his army across the border into oil-rich Kuwait. Kuwait was a major supplier of oil to the United States and a host of nations in Europe. The Iraqi takeover also posed near a certain threat to neighboring Saudi Arabia, another major exporter of oil.

MK V Special Operations Craft (SOC) underway; accompanied by two 11-meter NSW Rigid Inflatable Boats. Note the SEAL Combat Rubber Raiding Craft (CRRC) on the stern ramp of the MK V SOC.

Operation DESERT STORM, generally known as the first Gulf War, was a successful U.S.-Allied response to Iraq's attempt to overwhelm Kuwait. During this operation, Navy SEALs performed special reconnaissance and demolition missions up and down the Kuwaiti coastline in a prelude to a ground-war invasion. SDVs were also used to perform mine reconnaissance operations in areas where suspected minefields were thought to be located.

Before allied ground operations were initiated, a small group of SEALs swam undetected ashore from their combat rubber raiding craft and planted explosives along several hundred yards of the Kuwaiti shoreline. The timed detonation of these explosives, combined with extensive gunfire from the MK 5 Special Operations Craft by SWCC operators, was convincing enough to force Iraqi leaders to shift almost a division-sized force to defend the coast. They had been deceived into thinking that large amphibious invasion was forthcoming. This deception operation resulted in a U.S. Army and Marine Corps flanking operation coming over land from Saudi Arabia instead of by sea.

SEAL Delivery Vehicles (SDVs) were used to conduct pre-assault mine reconnaissance missions along the coast of Kuwait for Operation DESERT STORM.

SEALs successfully accomplished a variety of other missions on land, from the air, and from the sea during Operation DESERT STORM. Operations included: an assault using helicopters from a DDG that landed them on Qurah Island to conduct reconnaissance and sensitive site exploitation; visit, board, search, and size assaults against ships and small craft intending to lay mines; nighttime assaults against oil-drilling platforms and other infrastructures; and a mission that included infiltration into the desert to find and destroy a Tomahawk cruise missile that had failed to make its target and crashed.

Chapter 5:
Post 9/11/2001

Task Force K-BAR

On the morning of 11 September 2001, the United States suffered the greatest terrorist attack in its history, when four teams of al Qaeda terrorists hijacked four commercial airliners. Two planes crashed into the World Trade Center in New York City, a third plane crashed into the western side of the Pentagon, and a fourth plane, intended for the U.S. Capitol was instead crashed into a field in rural Pennsylvania. On 12 September, SEALs and other Special Operations Forces (SOF) were quickly deployed to a place they had not heretofore imagined – Afghanistan.

Combined Joint Special Operations Task Force K-BAR was given the mission to unilaterally destroy al Qaeda's ability to conduct operations throughout the country. Task Force K-BAR was under the command of Navy SEAL Captain Robert Harward. This extraordinary unit was comprised of Navy SEALs, USAF Combat Controllers, Army Special Forces, and SOF operators from seven nations: Joint Task Force 2 (Canada), the Australian Special Air Service Regiment, New Zealand Special Air Service, Kommando Spezialkräfte (Germany), Jægerkorpset og Frømandskorpset (Denmark), Jegerkommando og Marinejegerkommandoen (Norway), and Turkish Special Forces.

Task Force K-BAR immediately began focusing on strategic reconnaissance (SR) and direct action (DA) missions, which are core SEAL tasks. SR missions generally involved helicopter insertions of four-to-eight man elements that patrolled into tactical observation points. DA missions involved the capture or killing of high-value al Qaeda and Taliban leadership.

From October 2001 to April 2002, Task Force K-Bar carried out more than 75 missions, destroyed over 500,000 pounds of explosives and weapons, conducted sensitive site exploitation (SSE), and completed leadership interdiction missions that led to the killing of more than 115 Taliban and al Qaeda leaders and the capture 107 others. By April 2002, the Taliban government would be eliminated and the al Qaeda network in Afghanistan destroyed.

The men and women of Task Force K-BAR accomplished an unprecedented 100 percent mission success rate—a feat even more impressive given the wide variety of the missions. On 7 December 2004, President George W. Bush arrived at Camp Pendleton, California, and presented Task Force K-BAR the Presidential Unit Citation.

This U.S. Navy SEAL is seen conducting a strategic reconnaissance operation somewhere in Afghanistan. If enemy forces are observed, SEALs have the capability to laser-mark a target, while calling in tactical-air support equipped with precision-strike weapons.

Operation IRAQI FREEDOM

Naval Special Warfare SEALs, Special Warfare Combatant-craft Crewmen (SWCCs), and other Special Operations Forces played a widely expanded role in Operation IRAQI FREEDOM, where NSW men and women were instrumental in completing numerous special reconnaissance, direct action, and intelligence collection missions. Such missions included: the capture of the Al Faw peninsula oil infrastructures, clearing the Khawr Abd Allah and Khawr Zz Zubayr waterways, reconnaissance of the Shat Al Arab waterway, capture of high-value targets and high-value individuals, raids on suspected chemical, biological, and radiological sites, and the first POW rescue since World War II.

A U.S. Navy SEAL leading a daytime patrol somewhere in Afghanistan. They would approach the family in this picture to collect intelligence on enemy movement in the area of operation.

SEAL and Special Boat Team SWCCs from the Atlantic and Pacific were deployed on a rotational basis. SEAL Team THREE Delta Platoon arrived in Iraq in April 2006 with a mission to train Iraqi Army soldiers in Ramadi. Throughout the ensuing five months, the platoon engaged in combat with enemy forces in both day and nighttime operations. On 29 September, an enemy insurgent tossed a grenade at Petty Officer Michael Monsoor and several other SEALs that were positioned on a rooftop. Monsoor spotted the grenade and quickly smothered it with his entire body, thus, absorbing the resulting explosion, and saving his teammates from serious injury or death. Michael Monsoor lost his life during this courageous act, and was subsequently awarded the Medal of Honor. Also in his honor, the U.S. Navy will commission the *USS Michael Monsoor* (DDG-1001) sometime in the year 2016.

Operation ENDURING FREEDOM–Afghanistan

In May 2013, when he was the commander of the Naval Special Warfare Command in Coronado, California, Rear Admiral Sean Pybus announced that SEAL platoons in Afghanistan would be reduced by at least one half by the end of that year. He also stated that after being involved in mostly landlocked missions since 2001, Naval Special Warfare forces were already "undergoing a transition back to its maritime roots" by placing more emphasis on sea-based missions. The numbers of SEAL and other NSW personnel in Afghanistan have now been reduced even further.

After more than a decade in Afghanistan, the SEALs have experienced the best of times and also the worst. Certainly the most devastating period was during a quick-reaction force rescue operation on 28 June 2005 during Operation RED WINGS, when reconnaissance detachment of four SEALs, led by LT Michael Murphy, were ambushed several hours after being inserted by helicopter and patrolling some distance. Three of the four SEALs, including LT Murphy, were killed after a fierce gunfight. SEALs and other SOF aboard an MH-47 helicopter were scrambled to assist, and upon arrival at the remote mountain location, were shot down by an enemy with an RPG-7 (rocket propelled grenade), killing eight Navy SEALs and eight U.S. Army Special Operations aviation personnel on board. The *USS Michael Murphy* (DDG-112) was named in honor of LT Murphy, who was posthumously awarded the Medal of Honor.

Unquestionably, the pinnacle of success was during Operation NEPTUNE SPEAR, a cross-border CIA-led, interagency mission to capture or kill the world's foremost terrorist Osama bin Laden—the founder and head of the Islamist militant group al-Qaeda. He was killed in Pakistan on a mission launched from Afghanistan by U.S. Navy SEALs on 2 May 2011 shortly after 1:00 am.

This U.S. Navy SEAL is seen during daytime walk-through training before going out on a real-time mission. SEALs conduct numerous training rehearsals as they prepare for specifically assigned targets that are routinely accomplished at night.

Regretfully, the euphoria was short-lived, since another CH-47 Chinook helicopter, call sign Extortion 17, was shot down on 6 August 2011, while also transporting a quick-reaction force. These SEALs were attempting to reinforce Army Rangers engaged west of Kabul in Wardak province. The CH-47 crashed, killing all 38 men aboard, including 17 SEALs, five Army National Guard and Army Reserve air crewmen, seven Afghan commandos, one Afghan interpreter, and one combat-assault dog. This was the worst loss of U.S. military personnel in a single incident throughout the Afghanistan campaign and the largest single loss of NSW personnel on a single operation since the D-Day invasion at Normandy.

The Global War on Terrorism

While SEALs and other Special Operations Forces have reduced their activities in Afghanistan, the need for them has shifted to other parts of the world, where they and their military and inter-agency counterparts can be found operating in more than 70 countries. SEALs continue to target and eliminate terrorists and terrorist organizations in operations that remain highly classified. Many SEAL actions and activities have been discussed in an overabundance of movies, books, magazines, and television specials that often tend to over-glamorize these men, who are deployed day after day in arduous and dangerous conditions. These men make the nation proud, because they are truly the best at what they do. Many, however, have completed multiple combat rotations and the pressure on the force and stress on the families are beginning to take their toll.

Chapter 6:
Sea, Air, and Land Capabilities

How did SEALs become the foremost Maritime Special Operations force in the world? The history of developing and acquiring tactics, techniques, and equipment for SEALs began with many of their legacy-capability units from World War II. Men assigned to special mission or clandestine focused organizations tend to be creative and innovative, and these characteristics have been consistently displayed throughout the history of Naval Special Warfare.

The period early 1942 reflects a legacy of developments, innovations, and operating concepts surrounding maritime special operations that were driven by need and finding inventive ways to get the job done, since many of the mission tactics and techniques were being crafted as the war progressed.

The story of innovation and experimentation begins with the Atlantic naval demolition units, their basic and advanced training organization, the difficulties they encountered, and the ultimate success in mission accomplishment. These Naval Combat Demolition men were unique, because they had pre-assault demolition responsibilities on or near shore, and this was in contrast to the Pacific

Underwater Demolition Teams (UDTs), which were focused on pre-assault hydrographic reconnaissance and demolition of natural or man-made obstacles. The Atlantic units were among the first to operate in any theatre, thus, many problems they encountered and lessons learned proved helpful in determining training and policy in later operations. The Pacific UDTs evolved in much the same manner –through a lot of trial and error.

Two noteworthy WWII organizations were formed for formalized research, development, and experimentation involving maritime special operations. They were the Office of Strategic Services (OSS) in Washington, DC and the Joint Army-Navy Experimental and Testing (JANET) Board established 2 November 1942 and its Naval Demolition Research Unit (DRU) at Fort Pierce, Florida. The JANET mission was to "be responsible for the coordination of Army and Navy methods relative to the passage of obstacles in landing operations and for the testing of equipment and techniques in removal." It was also stipulated that JANET would maintain a close relationship with the OSS Maritime and Research Development Division.

Early photograph of SEAL Team TWO operators wearing camouflage uniforms.

Innovation was not restricted to the formalized developmental initiatives at JANET and the DRU. Undoubtedly, the earliest and most dynamic capability to come out of the field was the Hagensen Pack; an improvised demolition named after its innovator, Lieutenant Junior Grade Carl Hagensen, OIC of NCDU-30. While training in England, he conceived and developed a specialized explosive charge vital to elimination of Element "C" or Belgian Gate obstacles. They were used extensively on D-Day at the Normandy beaches, and the Hagensen Pack was improved some time later and became a standard explosive used by all of the military branches.

From a maritime perspective, most hardware innovations were realized by the OSS Maritime Unit; either through new designs or by modifying off-the-shelf systems to fit their needs. OSS activities created a steady demand for devices and documents that could be used to trick, attack, demoralize, or in any way exploit the enemy. MU worked with Dr. Chris Lambertsen to perfect the LARU pure-oxygen diving apparatus; developed specialized boats, equipment, and explosives; and fashioned things like fins, face masks, propelled submersibles, waterproof watches and compasses, inflatable motorized surfboards, and a two-man kayak.

In the Pacific, wide-ranging innovations were seen at the Naval Combat Demolition Training and Experimental Base established for UDT training at Maui, T.H., where virtually every early operation the UDT men conducted was an experiment; providing valuable lessons learned for training and on-going operations. The majority of UDT developments involved creation and refinement of operating tactics, techniques, and procedures rather than actually developing new hardware. It's why men engaged in combat and clad only in swim trunks with a K-Bar knife became known as the "naked warriors." The UDTs would benefit greatly during the post-war period by adopting OSS MU's tactics, techniques, and equipment.

UDT WWII Postwar Capabilities

During the postwar period, only the UDTs survived as established organizational units, where they became a doctrinal cornerstone of the still relatively new Amphibious Force. The period from 1945 through 1947 left the UDTs with little manpower and money with which to operate. Lieutenant Commander Francis Douglas "Red Dog" Fane, commander of the UDTs in the Atlantic Fleet, stands out as UDTs foremost innovator during this period. He successfully collaborated with Dr. Christian J. Lambertsen to employ his LARU, and quickly adopted the tactical combat-swimming methods used by the OSS Maritime Unit during WWII.

UDT-2 and UDT-4 began experimenting with the LARU and submersible "Sleeping Beauty" aboard the *USS Quillback* (SS-424) at St. Thomas, USVI in the spring of 1947 under the leadership of UDT Lieutenant Commander Fane. Training was directed by Dr. Lambertsen, who had been the OSS MU trainer and medical doctor during the war. The St. Thomas experiments resulted in formation of Submersible Operations platoons in the UDTs, simply called SUBOPS.

UDT operator Robert Gallagher and teammates preparing to dive the Draeger Lt. Lund II pure oxygen rebreather during training operations in the Mediterranean, circa 1957.

At the end of 1949, the Office of Naval Research and National Research Council collaborated by using scientific applications to address problems related to underwater diving. Their effort, which was largely focused on the UDTs, brought together operational, technical, civilian, and military subject-matter experts to conduct the "Cooperative Underwater Swimmer Project" ...to provide "attention on the primitive statue of knowledge in this area." UDT diving capabilities were studied extensively throughout the 1950s, because self-contained underwater breathing apparatus (SCUBA) were relatively new and much study needed to be accomplished. The UDTs were the first to employ compressed air for diving (SCUBA), which at the time was known as the Aqua-Lung commercially.

Tests were conducted at the Scripps Institution of Oceanography at San Diego State University with the full cooperation of UDT-1 and UDT-3. UDT men provided the support and manpower to serve as test subjects, while obtaining field data on swimmer performance in open-water conditions involving submerged diver and surface-swimmer operations. Studies resulting from the project that substantially impacted UDT capabilities included: open-circuit SCUBA diving tables, extensive O_2 breathing-gas studies, effects of explosives on divers with and without protective dress, and extended studies on diver-thermal protection to name a few. It was from this effort that rubber wet suits were invented.

During and after Korea, the UDTs had shifted almost entirely to use of open-circuit SCUBA, because of its ease of use. Soon, however, there was a great resurgence of activity to replace for the tactical LARUs, which were aging and could not be produced or supported. Tactical diving apparatus used by the UDTs during this period included the LS-901 Pirelli, manufactured by Pirelli, Milan, Italy and the Draeger Lt. Lund II, manufactured by Draegerwerk, Lüebeck, Germany. Both of these apparatus were difficult to maintain, thus, during the early 1960s, the UDTs migrated to Emerson pure-oxygen rebreather, manufactured in the U.S. by the J.H. Emerson Company as the standard tactical diving apparatus. They also adopted the MK VI semi-closed circuit diving, manufactured by the Scott Aviation Company of Buffalo, NY, which utilized a calculated pre-mixed percentage of nitrogen and oxygen that permitted the divers to go deep for longer periods of time and with fewer exhausted bubbles. Only

UDT and U.S. Navy Explosive Ordnance Disposal (EOD) divers used the MK VI, since it was designed to be low magnetic for operations in and around known and suspected mine fields. These diving apparatus remained the mainstay of UDT and SEAL operations until the 1970s, when the Emerson was eventually replaced with the pure-oxygen Draeger LAR III, made in Germany. The MK VI was replaced by the advanced-technology BioMarine CCR-1000 closed-circuit, mixed-gas underwater breathing apparatus which, in Navy jargon, became the MK 15 Underwater Breathing Apparatus (UBA). This was later replaced with the MK 16 UBA, which is a low-magnetic version of the MK 15, and used by SEAL delivery vehicle teamoperators and EOD diving units.

UDT and SEAL Air Operations–Helicopters

During the postwar period, the UDTs began experimenting with helicopters as a means to transport, launch, and recover swimmers, thus, providing them the potential for expanded sea-air operations. The UDT men would simply jump or be "cast" from a slowly moving helicopter flying very close to the water. They would be recovered with a winch or by climbing a caving ladder. In 1947, however, helicopter technology was relatively new and the Navy and Marine Corps versions didn't have the space or the lift capacity to allow development of a true operational capability. There is no evidence that helicopters provided routine training or operational capabilities that UDT could employ with the amphibious force.

This trend continued into the Korean War, where helicopters remained small and under-powered—picture the helicopters portrayed in the M*A*S*H television series. Larger and more powerful helicopters were emerging during the late 1950s and UDTs took advantage of the technology by developing helicopter cast and recovery techniques. The cast or launching of a swimmer was accomplished by mounting a swing bar outside of the helicopter. While the helicopter pilot was maintaining a speed equal to his altitude (e.g., 20 knots at 20 feet), the swimmer would grasp the bar and swing out of the helicopter while maintaining a rigid body position for water entry.

A rare photo of a UDT operator experimenting with helicopter cast and recovery techniques.

While practical methods of helicopter capabilities were being developed, the helicopter never became a mainstay for the UDTs, since boats remained the prime ship-to-shore mover for platoons of UDT men. The capability developed very quickly with the SEALs during the Vietnam period, since most operations were conducted on land and with smaller squad (six men) and platoon (12 men) sized elements. A variety of U.S. Army and Navy helicopters were often used for quick-strike raids and long-range insertion and extraction missions along the numerous rivers and canals of Vietnam's delta region and sometimes far inland. With the availability of powerful and reliable helicopters, the SEALs discovered many ways to employ them and their willing aircrews. Most noteworthy was how the SEALs worked very closely with U.S. Navy Seawolves Helicopter, Attack, Light or HAL detachments, which were often staged at the same base locations. Seawolves and SEALs were used together so successfully and so often that their operations became literally synonymous in the eyes of many local commanders.

Modern day SEALs use a variety of helicopters for short-range insertion and extraction, to conduct Visit, Board, Search, and Seize

(VBSS) operations using "Fast Roping" techniques, and to deliver them with their Combat Rubber Raiding Craft (CRRC). SEAL and Special Boat Teams have also developed operational capabilities with the Bell-Boeing V-22 Osprey; a multi-mission, tilt-rotor aircraft with both a vertical takeoff and landing and short takeoff and landing capabilities.

Navy SEALs conducting "Fast Rope" training from a UH-60 helicopter aboard a U.S. Navy warship.

The Special Patrol Insertion/ Extraction (SPIE) system provides the capability to rapidly extract SEALs from an area where it is difficult for helicopters to land. SPIE has application for rough terrain as well as water extractions. It could also be used for insertions; however, this would not be a preferred means tactically.

SEALs seen climbing into a CH-47 helicopter during day-time training operations.

UDT and SEAL Air Operations–Parachuting

It wasn't until after the Korean War that the UDTs began experimenting with parachutes. Of course the U.S. Army had a robust capability, but until the UDTs expanded their operations ashore in Korea, no one recognized that parachutes might provide greatly expanded capabilities.

In the Spring of 1950, five years after the close of World War II, and during the early period of the Korean War, the Chief of Naval Operations requested the commanders of Atlantic and Pacific Fleet UDTs to submit a list of UDT-qualified officers recommended for airborne training at Fort Benning, Georgia. As a result, in January 1951, a Lieutenant from UDT-2 was selected to attend. Upon graduation, he briefed the UDT commanders on the value of having Basic Airborne Training incorporated into the UDT program, both as a delivery means and to upgrade the quality of UDT training. A UDT-1 officer attended the next class and was followed by another from UDT-4.

Navy SEALs in a group formation steering toward a rally point in the water. SEALs have perfected this parachuting tactic and technique, where tactical operations are routinely accomplished under the cover of darkness from very high altitudes.

It is not clear if other UDT personnel attended parachuting training during the Korean War, but in 1954, while reviewing the UDT mission after the war, it was realized that the UDT mission directives contained wording stipulating that UDT should have the capability to be delivered to an objective area by parachute. This doctrinal statement was likely the result of recommendations made by UDT-1 and UDT-3 personnel during the early stages of the Korean War.

Quotas for 15 Atlantic Fleet UDT men were obtained from the Army in the spring of 1956. Their purpose was to complete Basic Airborne Training at Fort Benning, NC; and, upon return, to develop tactical water entry techniques. A call went out to both UDT-21 and

UDT-22 for volunteers, and virtually everyone signed up. Three officers and 12 enlisted men were selected. (Note: In 1954, UDT-1 and UDT-3 were re-designated UDT-11 and UDT-12 and UDT-2 became UDT-21. UDT-3 (formed for Korea) and UDT-22 were disestablished during the same period).

A Navy SEAL walking on water? Not really. This SEAL is making a water entry after jumping from high-altitude aboard a C-17 military aircraft. Tactically, the parachute will be ditched and allowed to sink in the ocean. The SEALs often use this capability to rendezvous with a U.S. Navy ship or submarine; used as an intermediate forward operating platform from which to launch tactical operations ashore or afloat.

The "dirty dozen plus three" were sent to Fort Benning for parachute training. Following graduation they remained an additional week for Jumpmaster Training, which included three more jumps. They also used this time to conduct experiments from the Army's 34-foot training towers wearing diver thermal protective dry suits and fins and facemasks, either worn or secured to the bellyband. Additional tests were accomplished with closed-circuit UBAs under the harness. This testing was accomplished in anticipation of making water-entry jumps once the men returned to Little Creek. Lack of funding to procure parachute equipment and a woeful lack of priority to schedule aircraft resulted in a four-year delay before any water jumps were actually conducted.

During the intervening years, additional quotas were sought so as to have a cadre of qualified personnel on board at all times. However, it was not until 1958 that 18 more quotas were obtained. Finally in 1960, it was concluded that delivery by parachute was a viable concept and that it should be formally incorporated into UDT tactical doctrine as an operational capability. At the same time, the UDTs were authorized an allowance of parachutes.

The SEAL Teams were among the first in the military to experiment with free-fall or high-altitude/low-opening (HALO) parachuting through their use of a parachute developed by the French in the mid-1960s. It was called the Para-Commander or PC, and was first used by sport parachute jumpers. The PC provided more control in the air once deployed, resulting in better accuracy and allowing the men to land at the same spot, thus improving tactical proficiency. As they did with the Army's static-line parachutes, SEALs took it upon themselves to develop and provide tactical water-entry tactics, techniques, and procedures. Once the capability was established, SEAL Team TWO was able to send most of their personnel through the Army's HALO School at Fort Benning, Georgia. SEAL Team ONE acquired the majority of their HALO training and qualifications at the Army's Yuma, Arizona Test Facility.

Today's SEALs use a para-foil or para-wing parachute that provides even more precision and better accuracy during tactical applications. Using these and similar parachutes, SEALs developed and perfected capabilities surrounding high-altitude/high-opening or HAHO (pronounced "Hay-HO"), which allow them to exit aircraft at altitudes of 36,000 feet, and where temperatures are extreme and sub-zero. HAHO operations require the use of supplemental oxygen, because of the extreme altitudes, and are very dangerous because of the potential for the men to experience hypoxia, which is a severe lack of oxygen.

SEALs and Research and Development

With establishment of the SEAL Teams in early 1962, and their parent Naval Operations Support Group (NOSG) Atlantic and Pacific staffs in 1963, formalized research and development programs for the UDT and SEAL Teams quickly followed. The NOSGs very early on established dedicated R&D Departments to coordinate acquisition of new and improved equipment and explosive devices that the fully involved the operators. Despite the somewhat greater formality of R&D today, the heritage of directly involving the men at operating teams in combat development on a day-to-day basis remains similarly focused, and especially at today's Naval Special Warfare Development Group, which has a robust Combat Development Division.

An early 1960s program called the Swimmer Underwater Reconnaissance and Clearance or SURAC project was expanded into two separate but related Specific Operational Requirements or SORs. These were the first formally established and funded research and development programs dedicated to the UDT and SEAL Teams. SOR 38-01 was called the Swimmer (later SEAL) Weapons System, and SOR 38-02 was called the Swimmer (later SEAL) Support System. From these were derived Technical Development Plans or TDPs using the same numbering systems, however, they were expanded to outline the technical parameters for the capabilities needed.

The SEAL Weapons System, TDP 38-01, was a long-range developmental program that listed 95 separate line items to be developed for the UDT and SEAL Teams over a period of several years. The SEAL Support System, TDP-38-02, was also a long-range program that outlined development of a Class I and Class II SDV, Class I and Class II Underwater Breathing Apparatus (UBA), and a host of ancillary equipment. The TDP also called for conversion of the two Regulus II cruise-missile carrying submarines, *USS Grayback* (SSG-574) and *USS Growler* (SSG-577), to host, launch, and recover SDVs. The *Grayback* was converted and deployed in the Pacific to support SDV operations. The *Growler* was never converted owing to lack of funding.

Deck crews preparing to recover a MK VIII SEAL Delivery Vehicle (SDV) during training operations aboard a nuclear submarine.

The Class I UBA was a closed-circuit, pure-oxygen diving apparatus, and it was satisfied by the German Draeger LAR III UBA, which remains in use today as the MK 25, Mod 2. The Class II UBA was a closed-circuit, mix-gas rebreather, which was a very high technology diving apparatus that remains in service today as the MK 16, Mod 1 UBA. The MK 16 is used exclusively by the SDV Team because of its ability to operate at deeper depths for longer durations, allowing significant mission capabilities--many of which remain classified.

From the early 1960s until formation of the United States Special Operations Command (USSOCOM) in 1987, much of the research and development activity revolved around improving or modernizing capabilities already in the SEAL Team inventory. Once USSOCOM was organized, all U.S. Navy sponsorship surrounding research, development, and acquisition for the SEAL and Special Boat Teams migrated to the command's headquarters in Tampa, FL. Many of the SEAL unique programs were executed by the Naval Special Warfare Program Office at the Naval Sea Systems Command in Washington, DC, and many were continued there under USSOCOM sponsorship.

SEAL and Special Boat Capabilities

There was nothing special about the boats used to transport the Naval Combat Demolition Units at Normandy and Southern France in 1944. They were taken ashore by ship's company, where they operated out of inflatable rubber boats laden with explosives. They were taken near shore in a variety of naval craft and from a variety of Navy ships.

In the Pacific, the UDTs operated their own boats for training and during combat operations. They used LCPRs (Landing Craft Personnel, Ramp) carried by specially outfitted Amphibious, Personnel Destroyers or APDs. The LCPRs were used to transport inflatable boats, which were used by the men to get closer to the beach. The inflatable rubber boat was also used in conjunction with the LCPRs to drop and pick up swimmers at high speeds.

Throughout the war, the APDs and UDTs operated as a tight family unit. This was the first and only time in the history of Naval Special Warfare that ships were totally dedicated to the men for combat use. APDs were also used by the UDTs in the Korean War, but they were never again totally dedicated platforms.

Four UDTs were formed after World War II, and they maintained what became a doctrinal custom of owning and operating their own LCPRs and later the newer LCPLs (Landing Craft, Personnel, Large). When the UDT platoons began overseas deployment as part of an Amphibious Ready Group, their boats were loaded aboard ship and taken with them on the cruise.

Early in the Vietnam War, the SEALs had no dedicated boat support and were substantially hampered by what little Navy support existed. They used steel-hull MK 4 LCPLs modified extensively with gun mounts, radar, and protective sun shields. They also used the Navy river patrol boats (Patrol Boat, Riverine or PBRs). Members of SEAL Team TWO adapted a commercially produced fiber-glass boat with out-board motors that provided much higher speeds, and were equipped with several gun mounts. These were called SEAL Team Assault Boats or STABs, but very few were ever deployed.

The Light SEAL Support Craft (LSSC) above, and the Medium SEAL Support Craft (MSSC) below, were designed and built for SEAL operations in Vietnam. These were the first boats specifically designed by the Navy for Naval Special Warfare operations.

In the late 1960s, a hasty craft development program was established in Washington to procure boats specially designed for SEAL riverine operations. These were the Light SEAL Support Craft (LSSC) and Medium SEAL Support Craft (MSSC). The LSSC was a squad-sized boat with water-jet propulsion and a exceptionally small draft that could get into very shallow water regions. The MSSC was a platoon-sized boat that was also propelled by water jets. It had a shallow draft and a top speed of over about 35 knots. None of these craft were returned to the United States after the war. The MSSCs were eventually replaced with better-designed craft called the Mini Armored Troop Carrier (ATC). The Mini-ATC was designed as a replacement for the MSSC during the Vietnam War, but arrived too late to serve in Vietnam. They were distributed to the Coastal River Divisions and later the Special Boat Units. During the late 70s and up to the 90s they were the primary boat used for Riverine operations and SEAL platoon support. The Naval Special Warfare Special Boat Units became the repository of many Vietnam era boats--for the most part the Mini-ATCs and PBRs were largely operated and maintained by Vietnam veteran's in the reserve components.

The UDTs continued to use the MK-4 and MK-11 LCPLs for ship-to-shore movement, however, the Navy decided to quite acquiring these craft, and this led NSW toward development of the Special Warfare Combatant Craft, Light (SWCCL) also known as the SEAFOX. The boat had a unique design and considerable operational deficiencies with both good and bad reviews. As one special boat veteran commented, "The boat looked very spooky to foreigners, so we had to get special permission to launch it almost everywhere we went."

SEAFOX under way

A continuation of problems eventually resulted in replacing the SEAFOX with the 11-meter NSW Rigid Hull Inflatable Boat (RHIB or RIB).

An 11-meter NSW rigid hull inflatable boat (RHIB) descends to the water using Maritime Craft Aerial Deployment System (MCADS). Special Warfare Combatant-craft crewmen (SWCC) free-fall jump after the RHIB, and prepare to get underway once they reached the water. U.S. Navy photo by Chief Mass Communication Specialist Kathryn Whittenberger (Released)

SEALs and their UDT forefathers have always used some form of inflatable boats operationally. SEALs currently use the F-470 Zodiac or Combat Rubber Raiding Craft (CRRC) as a primary over-the-beach tactical insertion craft. They also launch and recover CRRCs from Navy, Army, and USAF aircraft using a variety of techniques. The NSW 11-meter RIB operated by the SWCCs was sized to support a SEAL squad. It can be delivered worldwide and parachuted into the sea using its Maritime Craft Aerial Delivery System or MCADS from fixed-with aircraft. Another boat, the Special Operations Craft, Riverine (SOCR), which eventually replaced the Mini-ATC and PBR missions, can be launched and recovered by the CH-47 helicopter. New and more capable craft are currently being designed and procured to replace the current generation of NSW special boats.

Navy SEAL *Ethos*

In times of war or uncertainty there is a special breed of warrior ready to answer our Nation's call. A common man with uncommon desire to succeed. Forged by adversity, he stands alongside America's finest special operations forces to serve his country, the American people, and protect their way of life. I am that man.

My Trident is a symbol of honor and heritage. Bestowed upon me by the heroes that have gone before, it embodies the trust of those I have sworn to protect. By wearing the Trident I accept the responsibility of my chosen profession and way of life. It is a privilege that I must earn every day. My loyalty to Country and Team is beyond reproach. I humbly serve as a guardian to my fellow Americans always ready to defend those who are unable to defend themselves. I do not advertise the nature of my work, nor seek recognition for my actions. I voluntarily accept the inherent hazards of my profession, placing the welfare and security of others before my own. I serve with honor on and off the battlefield. The ability to control my emotions and my actions, regardless of circumstance, sets me apart from other men. Uncompromising integrity is my standard. My character and honor are steadfast. My word is my bond.

We expect to lead and be led. In the absence of orders I will take charge, lead my teammates and accomplish the mission. I lead by example in all situations. I will never quit. I persevere and thrive on adversity. My Nation expects me to be physically harder and mentally stronger than my enemies. If knocked down, I will get back up, every time. I will draw on every remaining ounce of strength to protect my teammates and to accomplish our mission. I am never out of the fight.

We demand discipline. We expect innovation. The lives of my teammates and the success of our mission depend on me – my technical skill, tactical proficiency, and attention to detail. My training is never complete. We train for war and fight to win. I stand ready to bring the full spectrum of combat power to bear in order to achieve my mission and the goals established by my country. The execution of my duties will be swift and violent when required yet guided by the very principles that I serve to defend. Brave men have fought and died building the proud tradition and feared reputation that I am bound to uphold. In the worst of conditions, the legacy of my teammates steadies my resolve and silently guides my every deed. I will not fail.

Plaque honoring U.S. Navy SEALs dedicated at the U.S. Navy Memorial, Washington, DC on 15 June 2002.

References

1.   Bosiljevac, T.L. *SEALs: UDT-SEAL Operations in Vietnam.* New York: Ballantine Books. 1990.

2.   Cooper, Marvin. *The Men from Fort Pierce: A Chronological Survey of the Underwater Demolition Teams of World War II.* Manuscript undated and self-published.

3.   Dunford, Sue Ann and O'Dell, James Douglas. *More Than Scuttlebutt: The U.S. Navy's Demolition Men in World War II.* 2009. (ISBN 978-0-615-30664-3).

4.   Dwyer, John B. *Scouts and Raiders: The Navy's First Naval Special Warfare Commandos.* New York: Praeger Publishers. 1993.

5.   Ibid. *Commandos From the Sea: The History of Amphibious Special Warfare in World War II and the Korean War.* Paladin Press. 1968.

6.   Fane, Commander Francis Douglas and Moore, Don. *The Naked Warriors.* Appleton-Century-Crofts, Inc. 1956.

7.   Gawne, Jonathan. *Spearheading D-Day: American Special Units of the Normandy Invasion.* Historire & Collections, Paris, France. 1998.

8.   *History of the OSS Maritime Unit.* Found in National Archives. Compiled and published by the OSS.

9.   Fields, James A. *History of the United States Naval Operations: Korea.* Washington, DC: Government Printing Office. 1962.

10.   Haas, Michael E. *In the Devil's Shadow: U.N. Special Operations During the Korean War.* U.S. Naval Institute Press. 2002.

11.   Hoyt, Edwin P. *SEALs at War.* New York: Bantam Doubleday Dell Publishing Group, Inc. 1993.

12.   Lynch, Grayson L. *Decision for Disaster: Betrayal at the Bay of Pigs.* Brassey's: Dulles, VA. 1998.

13.   History Project, Strategic Services Unit, Office of the Assistant Secretary of War, War Department, Washington, DC. *War Report of the OSS (Office of Strategic Services).* Walker and Company. 1976.

14.   Triay, Victor Andres. *Bay of Pigs: An Oral History of Brigade 2504.* University Press of Florida. 2001.

15.   Staudt, Theresa and Staudt, Henry, *Hidden Heroes: The Story of Special Services Unit #1*, Self-published, undated, and presented to the Navy History and Heritage Command, circa 1999.

About the Author

Commander Tom Hawkins retired from the U.S. Navy after 24-years active service as a career SEAL and Naval Special Warfare (NSW) officer. He completed operational tours in Underwater Demolition Team 21 and SEAL Team TWO, where he deployed to the Republic of Vietnam as a Platoon Commander. He commanded UDT-22 for 33 months and accomplished its reorganization and establishment as SEAL Delivery Vehicle Team TWO. After assignment as Chief Staff Officer, Naval special Warfare Group TWO he served on the NSW staff in the Pentagon. At the time of his Navy retirement he was Director, NSW Programs at the Naval Sea Systems Command in Washington, DC.

After leaving the Navy Tom served in various technical support positions related to NSW and the SEAL and Special Boat Teams. Most recently he served as an Acquisition and Requirements Analyst and Policy and Programs Advisor at the Naval Special Warfare Development Group. He retired from NSWDG on 30 May 2014.

Between 1995 and 2005 Tom served as president of the UDT-SEAL Association, president of the UDT-SEAL Memorial

Park Association, and on the Board of Directors at the UDT-SEAL Museum Association. In the year 2000 he was founding president and chairman of the Naval Special Warfare Foundation, where he also served as Director, History and Heritage. From 1994 until 2005, he was editor of "The BLAST" – the magazine "Journal of Naval Special Warfare," published quarterly by the UDT-SEAL Association and Naval Special Warfare Foundation (now Navy SEAL Foundation).

Tom is the Chairman and Chief Executive Office of Phoca Press, which is dedicated to publishing works by, for, and about the Naval Special Warfare community. Phoca's mission is to enhance the public's appreciation and understanding of the contributions of NSW through a wide array of history and heritage projects.

PHOCA
P r e s s ✺ L L C

www.PhocaPress.com
New York, NY 10025

Design and Layout: Lisa Merriam

Edited by Tom Hawkins and Lisa Merriam

Copy Editor: Patrick Roye